I0447637

NEUROIMMUNE MEDIATED –

OBSESSIVE COMPULSIVE DISORDER

(NM-OCD)

By

Dr. Christian R. Komor

OCD Recovery Center of America

NEUROIMMUNE-MEDIATED OBSESSIVE COMPULSIVE DISORDER

© 2012 by Christian R. Komor

All material in this book is, unless otherwise stated, the property of Dr. Christian R. Komor. Copyright and other intellectual property laws protect these materials. Reproduction or retransmission of the materials, in whole or in part, in any manner, without the prior written consent of the copyright holder, is a violation of copyright law.

A single copy of the materials available through this course may be made, solely for personal, noncommercial use. Individuals must preserve any copyright or other notices contained in or associated with them. Users may not distribute such copies to others, whether or not in electronic form, whether or not for a charge or other consideration, without prior written consent of the copyright holder of the materials. Contact information for requests for permission to reproduce or distribute materials available through this course are listed below: Christian R. Komor, Psy.D., OCD Recovery Center, P.O. Box 6654, Grand Rapids, MI 49516

Library of Congress Cataloging in Publication Data

Komor, Christian R., 1959-
    Neuroimmune Mediated Obsessive Compulsive Disorder

By Christian R. Komor.
                p.   cm.

includes bibliographic references.
1. Anxiety 2. Self-Help

I. Title.

RC569.5.WW67K66   1992

616.85'2 – dc20   92-13568

SBN-13: 978-1478285359

ISBN-10: 1478285354

Publisher: KEI GLOBAL
               P.O. Box 6025
               Grand Rapids, Michigan 49516
               www.keiglobal.com

DEDICATION

This book is dedicated with an apology to all those OCD patients who are suffering with undiagnosed or untreated NM-OCD; especially those children whose neuro-immune systems are being further damaged through long-term antibiotics and psychotropic drugs. We could have diagnostic tools and interventions in hand already if research dollars were being used with intelligence and insight. Hopefully this book and others like it will begin to change this situation.

CONTENTS

A PROFESSIONALINTRODUCTION.............Page 6

A PERSONAL INTRODUCTION.........…......Page 8

THE PROBLEM OF OBSESSIVE COMPULSIVE DISORDERS........................Page 12

PSYCHONEUROIMMUNOLOGY AND OBSESSIVE COMPULSIVE SPECTRUM DISORDERS…......Page 15

INFECTIOUS DISEASE AND OBSESSIVE COMPULSIVE SPECTRUM DISORDERS…......Page 18

IMMUNE SYSTEM, CYTOKINES AND THE BRAIN....................…........Page 24

IMMUNE SYSTEM DYSFUNCTION IN OCD.............................…..Page 26

THE BLOOD-BRAIN BARRIER (BBB) AND ITS PERMEABILITY.............…...Page 29

NEURONEUROIMMUNE MEDIATED OCD (NM-OCD)...............................Page 32

DIAGNOSTIC AND TREATMENT INNOVATIONS.....................….............Page 37

DISCUSSION AND GENERAL RECOMMENDATIONS...........................Page 68

A FINAL COMMENTARY.......................…...Page 71

REFERENCES...................…....….........Page 72

A PROFESSIONAL INTRODUCTION

"There is one thing even more vital to science than intelligent methods; and that is, the sincere desire to find out the truth, whatever it may be." - Charles Pierce

Now known to be a relatively common (2-3% prevalence), genetically determined disorder of the cortical-thalamic-striatal (CTS) circuitry of the brain, Obsessive Compulsive Disorder (OCD) can be a devastating brain illness which continues to place a heavy burden on the healthcare system in spite of the development of 5HT reuptake blocking medications which are partially effective (roughly 30% improvement in 60% of patients without placebo effect) in reducing the symptoms of OCD. The serotonergic hypothesis has come under challenge from an array of more contemporary invitro and invivo studies indicating involvement of dopaminergic, inositol second messenger, glutamatergic, autoimmune and other mechanisms in the pathogenisis of OCD. Following in the footsteps of several of the neuro-immune-mediated (NMD) degenerative disorders such as Multiple Sclerosis, Parkinson's disease, and Alzheimer's Disease and particularly Sydenham's Chorea, strong evidence now implicates dysregulation of the immune system in the activation and maintenance of many forms of OCD. It is postulated that approaching OCD as a potentially Neuroimmune Mediated disorder may allow for the application of   already-existing diagnostic and treatment innovations already in use in collateral field as well as the development of new treatment methodologies in specific to Neuroimmune Mediated Obsessive Compulsive Disorders (NM-OCD)

In this monograph on Neuroimmune Mediated Obsessive Compulsive Disorder (NM-OCD) our hope is to bring to light correlations between research derived from studies of other neurological disorders such as Parkinson's Disease, MS, and Alzheimer's and our own field of Obsessive Compulsive Disorders. In the paper we explore existing research in psychoneuroimmunology, blood - brain barrier dysfunction, and anti-neuronal processes in the brain. Based on this data we formulate a number of conclusions and recommendations.

This monograph, then, puts forward the following hypotheses as applied to the OCSD field:

(1)   The current chasm between controlled research and clinical application must be bridged.

(2)   Critical breakthroughs in OCSD treatment await at the intersection of immunology,   neurology, endocrinology, genetics, psychopharmacology, and psychology.

(3)   Psychoneuroimmunological findings with pediatric and adult OCD patients may have some   degree of applicability to other Obsessive Compulsive Spectrum Disorders.

A PERSONAL INTRODUCTION

"A man's interest in a single bluebird is worth more than a complete but dry list of the fauna and flora of a town." - Henry David Thoreau

It is still hard to talk about the birth of my own Obsessive Compulsive Disorder (OCD) which coincided with the birth of my son in 1994. Born prematurely at 24 weeks gestational age, his mother and I spent close of four months watching over him with anxious intensity in a Neonatal Intensive Care Unit. Quickly trained by the NICU staff to obsessive levels of hand washing, germ avoidance, hyper-cleanliness, and attention to the detail of every tube, wire, lead and sensor and monitor, my genetic predisposition to OCD awoke with a fury (very personal evidence of the "diathesis stress" or "two hit" theory of neuropsychological disease development). Soon cracks in the tile, buttons on the telephone, and doorways all became temptations for my brain to lock onto and try and control. As I received my own OCD diagnosis I found myself turning my decades years of training and experience as a clinical psychologist toward the quest for optimal solutions to my own predicament – and those of my OCD patients who were rapidly growing in number.

A voracious reader of controlled research studies, I became aware that my son might have inherited a genetic susceptibility for the disorder as well. Indeed, in the winter of 1999 OCD again visited our little family as my son was plunged into an acute episode of obsessions and rituals following a streptococcal infection. The happy and carefree boy we had fought so hard to save was suddenly frozen in the bathroom unable to complete heretofore mundane tasks. Simple decisions became overwhelmingly complex reached only on the far side of a long agonizing process. Urinary control was lost. Order and organization took the place of play and enjoyment. The most amazing element of the situation for me was how rapidly the change had occurred – literally overnight! Social-emotional problems, I was aware, simply did not act lik this. Fortunately, compared to the fate of many including myself, the resolution for our son was also rapid – due in part to swift action by my wife and I and the courage to trust science and research. Against the urging of our well-meaning physicians and even the National Institutes of Mental Health we dug deep into our own pockets and courage and located a physician willing to provide our son with an infusion of intravenous immunoglobulin (IVIG). Within days we found we had engineered almost immediate 40-50% reduction in symptoms. Time did the rest of the healing and by the end of that troubled year our son was 90% back to his happy, carefree self.

Now known to be a relatively common disorder of the cortical-thalamic-striatal (CTS) circuitry of the brain, OCD was only a few years ago considered a rare, treatment refractory disorder of psychological origin (probably resulting from poor toilet training in childhood or other parental depredations). In large, multicentre, double-blind, placebo-controlled studies physicians found that serotonergic medications that blocked reuptake such as Clomiprimine, fluoxetine, fluvoxemine, paroxetine, sertraline and citalopram were all mildly effective (roughly 30% improvement in 60% of patients) treatments for OCD. Contrasting pharmacological challenges with specific serotonin agonists such as mCPP and sumatriptan were associated with transient exacerbation of OCD symptoms – leading to the serotonergic hypothesis of OCD. Soon, however, it became apparent that this serotonergic hypothesis, while necessary, was hardly in itself sufficient. Emerging studies and the lack of compelling clinical result made it clear that there was more to the understanding and treatment of OCD than met the eye. Dopaminergic, inositol second messenger, glutamatergic, autoimmune and other mechanisms have all come under scrutiny and thousands of research studies have ensued – yet the treatment standard for OCD remains as it was decades ago – serotonergic medication and behavioral therapy. We need to do better. In particular we need to do a better job of employing *already available* research to create more optimized treatment outcomes.

Surveying the literature and reviewing empirical data from this author's treatment of hundreds of Obessive Compulsive Spectrum Disorder patients and training of thousands of providers in the field, the specter of *neuroimmune involvement* arises with such frequency and clarity and intensity that it is difficult not to ascribe some degree of face validity. Indeed, piecing together a broad overview of the literature with a broad sampling of patients a pattern emerges – a cascade of events beginning with the immune system, penetrating and traversing the blood-brain barrier, stimulating the development of anti-neuronal antibodies in genetically susceptible regions of the brain (e.g. basal ganglia, hippocampus) and disrupting the neurochemical and structural mirocenvironment of the central nervous system. It is the hypotheses of this monograph that not only should the lingering question of "Do immune events play a role in Obsessive Compulsive Spectrum Disorders?" receive long-overdue affirmation, but that the role of neuroimmune events in these disorders may be far greater than has been suspected. It is our hypothesis that, viewed in a linear distribution, neuroimmune events play no role in perhaps 10-20% of pediatric *and* adult OCD patients, a pivotal role in the same percentage, and at least some role in the remaining 60-80% of patients. While impossible to even hypothesize at present, data suggest neuroimmune involvement in some variation and degree in many of the Obsessive Compulsive Spectrum Disorders (see below). If this hypothesis of Neuroimmune involvement is correct a field of new options for treatment opens itself for exploration.

Dr. Christian R. Komor

July, 2012

THE PROBLEM OF OBSESSIVE COMPULSIVE DISORDER

"What is a scientist after all? It is a curious man looking through a keyhole, the keyhole of nature, trying to know what's going on." - Jacques Yves Cousteau

Obsessive Compulsive Disorder (OCD) is a significantly handicapping brain illness which carries a large medical and social burden. Ranked among the top ten most disabling medical conditions by the World Health Organization, two to five billion dollars are spent in the North America each year for medical costs related to OCD with six billion dollars more in lost productivity.

To date, however, treatment outcomes are lackluster at best and leave the majority of patients in substantial discomfort. (Denys et al, 2004). While hundreds of research studies related to Obsessive Compulsive Spectrum Disorders have emerged especially in the two decades, cognitive-behavioral counseling and serotonergic medications are the only widely recognized treatment strategies. Each show only 30% improvement in 60% of patients for the tormenting obsessions and exhausting compulsive behaviors suffered by patients with OCD. But in a significant cross-section of OCD patients, cognitive-behavioral and serotonin-modifying interventions seem to be overwhelmed by additional physiologic or environmental forces which inhibit meaningful recovery. Even among cohorts receiving active treatment, levels of disability in work, relationships and activities of daily living remains in the 50% range. (Franklin ME, Foa EB 2011).

Obsessive compulsive disorders tend to be highly disabling and carry a significant social burden. Two to five billion dollars are spent in the US each year for medical costs related to OCD alone with six billion dollars more in lost productivity. OCD is ranked among the top ten most disabling medical conditions by the World Health Organization. Treatment outcomes are incomplete. Less than 60% of patients receive less than 30% benefit from standard medication regimes and similar statistics result from behavior interventions. (Denys et al 2004). While thousands of research studies related to Obsessive Compulsive Spectrum Disorders have been conducted in the past 30 years (most in the last 10) behavioral counseling and serotonergic medications are the only recognized treatment strategies that have emerged with the aforementioned limited results in improving patient quality of life.

The boundaries between Obsessive Compulsive Disorder (OCD) and other neuropsychiatric disorders remain unresolved and may well differ from one disorder to another. Endophenotypes are heritable, quantitative traits hypothesized to more closely represent genetic risk for complex polygenic mental disorders than overt symptoms and behaviors. They may have a role in identifying how closely these disorders are associated with another and with other mental disorders with which they share major comorbidity. Similarities in phenomenology, comorbidity, familial and genetic features, brain circuitry, and treatment response between OCD and several related disorders characterized by repetitive thoughts or behaviors suggest that they may be grouped for the purposes of diagnosis and treatment. The disorders that have been examined for inclusion in the DSM-V included OCD, obsessive-compulsive personality disorder (OCPD), Tourette's syndrome (TS) and other tic disorders, Sydenham's chorea, Pediatric Autoimmune Neuropsychiatric Disorders Associated with Streptococcal Infections (PANDAS), Trichotillomania (TTM), Body Dysmorphic Disorder (BDD), Autism, Eating Disorders, Huntington's and Parkinson's disease, impulse control disorders, as well as substance and behavioral addictions.

For the purposes of this monograph The Obsessive Compulsive Best Practices Foundation (OCBPF) feels confident that OCD, BDD, OCPD, TS, TTM, and Compulsive Hoarding share enough commonalities on the aforementioned parameters to warrant inclusion on an Obsessive Compulsive Spectrum of Disorders (OCDS).

PSYCHONEUROIMMUNOLOGY AND OBSESSIVE COMPULSIVE SPECTRUM DISORDERS

The immune system is now considered a diffuse sensory organ and regulator of metabolism which works in concert with the nervous system to achieve and maintain homeostasis throughout the body. Immunocompetent cells are located throughout the body in virtually every organ – including the brain. Sophisticated and highly complex interactions that are both health enhancing and health detracting occur among these cells. In the main these interactions are orchestrated by soluble protein messengers called *cytokines* of which there are many different varieties. Cytokines are produced in the brain during normal development and function, but are expressed at much higher levels in response to *infection or damage*. It appears that increased cytokine exposure during key periods of brain development may act as a "vulnerability" factor for later-life development of neuro-behavioral pathology by sensitizing the neuronal system (Bilbo and Schwarz, 2009). It would appear that even influenza or bacterial infections such as *E. coli* can induce cytokine production by the maternal immune system, the fetal immune system, and the placenta (Hillier et al, 1993) or at later stages in human development (Hagberg and Mallard, 2005)

The interactions between the immune and central nervous systems (CNS) in pathological states such as multiple sclerosis and depression have long been under investigation. In recent years, the discovery of multiple functions of cytokines in the central nervous system suggests that cytokines play a central role in complex CNS functions including cognition (Hopkins and Rothwell, 1995; Pollmacher et al., 2002; Rothwell, 1999; Rothwell and Hopkins, 1995; Wilson et al., 2002). Indeed, the over-expression of cytokines has been associated with numerous pathological states (both within the central and peripheral nervous system), such as infection (viral, bacterial and fungal), autoimmune disease (i.e. multiple sclerosis), stroke, trauma, neurodegenerative disease (i.e. Alzheimer's disease (AD) and other dementias) (Rothwell and Loddick, 2002; Shaftel et al., 2008) and in neuropsychiatric disorders, such as depression (Capuron and Dantzer, 2003; Kronfol and Remick, 2000; Raison et al., 2006). Some cytokines, such as interleukin 1beta (IL-1-beta), interleukin 6 (IL-6) and tumor necrosis factor (TNF) have been associated with cognitive decline and dementia including Alzheimer's Disease (TNF and IL-1-beta) in several cross-sectional and prospective population studies (Dik et al., 2005; Holmes et al., 2003; Schmidt et al., 2002).

Most researchers believe that microglia derive from mesodermal precursors infiltrating blood monocytes during pre- and postnatal life. *Microglia are the primary immuncompetent cells of the brain* and are present in every major aspect of brain development, function and disease (Barres, 2008). In response to injury or stimulation, microglia become considerably more active and upregulate a number of surface receptors producing the cytokines which in turn influence neuronal function. While microglia serve helpful functions in the nervous system, excessive activation of the microglia is correlated with multiple neuroinflammatory and neurodegenerative disorders (e.g.

Parkinson's, Multiple Sclerosis, Alzheimer's Disease, Huntington's Disease) (Perry, 2004).

It is important to note that although the increased levels of cytokines seen in patients with OCSD may be detrimental to neuroplasticity, certain levels of pro-inflammatory cytokines are essential for normal brain development and homeostatic regulation of synaptic scaling (Avital et al. 2003; Beattie et al. 2002; Goshen et al. 2007, 2008; Stellwagen & Malenka, 2006). These two conflicting pieces of evidence suggest that it may be the *disturbance of this intricate equilibrium between physiological and pathophysiolgical levels of cytokines* in the brain that affects synaptic plasticity and plays a critical role in the pathophysiology of MDD.

Functional imaging studies have reported with remarkable consistency hyperactivity in the orbitofrontal cortex (OFC), anterior cingulate cortex (ACC), and caudate nucleus of patients with obsessive-compulsive disorder (OCD). Converging evidence from these various lines of research supports a causal role for the cortico-basal ganglia-thalamo-cortical loops that involve the OFC and ACC in the pathogenesis of OCD in children and adults. Cytokine receptors are distributed throughout the brain with their highest concentrations are in the hippocampal region and basal ganglia.

INFECTIOUS DISEASE AND OBSESSIVE COMPULSIVE SPECTRUM DISORDERS

Syphilis, Lyme Disease, vascular disorders, tumors, and neurodegenerative disease processes such as Parkinson's Disease, Huntington's Chorea, Lupus and Multiple Sclerosis are all well-known to cause primary and, or secondary psychological effects. As far back as 1929 Selling presented a case series and inferred the possibility of an infection precipitating tics. Zabriskie et al (1978) first identified *antineuronal antibodies* in Sydenham's chorea. These antibodies recognized calls within the subthalamic and caudate nuclei and were absorbed by streptococcal cellular components. (These findings are consistent with the concept of molecular mimicry - cross-reactivity between antigens in disease-associated streptococci and brain proteins.)

During the last few years, an increased interest in the possibility of *immune mediated pathophysiology* of Obsessive Compulsive Disorder and related disorders has emerged. Several lines of accumulating evidence support neuroimmunologic involvement to one degree or another in several of the aforementioned Obsessive Compulsive Spectrum Disorders. The temporal association between increased prevalence of OCD in patients with *rheumatic fever (RF)*, and the aggregation of obsessive-compulsive spectrum disorders among relatives of RF probands is suggestive. In 1994 Kiessling, Marcotte and Culpepper at Brown University conducted fluorescent serum antibody assessments of a group of children with OCD and their healthy controls. The sera from clinical cases showed antibodies directed against caudate, putamen, or both providing evidence of basal ganglia involvement in OCSD.

In the same year Roy et al at the VA Medical Center in Albany, New York reported on patients with obsessive-compulsive disorder (OCD) who demonstrated significant levels of antibody for somatostatin-28, its C-terminal fragment somatostatin-14, and prodynorphin with contrasting lower levels of reactivity for somatostatin-28(1-14) (the N-terminal fragment of somatostatin-28) and negligible reactivity for several other peptides including beta-endorphin and corticotropin. (Healthy volunteers and disease controls [schizophrenia, Alzheimer's disease, multiple sclerosis, and subjects with advanced human immunodeficiency virus (HIV) infection] exhibited negligible reactivity.) The researchers concluded that, "These data raise the consideration of an autoimmune mechanism for some forms of OCD."

Other early researchers found no (Black et al, 1998) or limited (Moer et al, 1999) correlation between markers of autoimmunity and OCD.

Group A Streptococcal Infection (GAS), Rheumatic Fever and Syndenham's Chorea

Research and practice related to the neuroimmunological characteristics of Obsessive Compulsive Spectrum Disorders has been limited in populations and disease processes studied. This limited view of autoimmune mediated obsessive compulsive disorders as confined to streptococcal infections probably arose from an over-application of the template of Sydenham's chorea (a choreaform disorder arising in the aftermath of acute rheumatic fever (ARF) which in turn is triggered by group A beta-hemolytic streptococcal infections. ARF consists of several combinations of carditis, polyarthritis and Sydenham's chorea, and rarely seen erythema marginatum and subcutaneous nodules. Sydenham's chorea appears in about 20% of patients with ARF. As a late symptom of ARF, Sydenham's chorea usually occurs 3 months or longer after the streptococcal infection.

Sydenham's chorea is a neuropsychiatric disorder that may present with emotional lability, anxiety, obsessive compulsive symptoms, attention deficit and hyperactivity symptoms or tics. Obsessive-compulsive symptoms occur in 70% of patients with Sydenham's chorea. Two main types of immunological changes have been described in patients with Syndenham's Chorea: (1) presence of *antineuronal antibodies* in serum CSK and (2) changes in host *B-lymphocyte markers* such as tumor necrosis factor alpha - a *proinflammatory cytokine* involved in several autoimmune diseases. Researchers have found that polymorphisms in the promoter region of the TNFA gene have been associated with RF.

In 1995 researchers at the National Institute of Mental Health (Allen et al, 1995) reported increased levels of obsessive compulsive symptoms in patients with Sydenham chorea (SC). Obsessive-compulsive symptoms occur in 70% of patients with Sydenham's chorea. The role of autoimmune mechanisms and the dysfunction of the basal ganglia have been demonstrated in Sydenham's chorea – thus demonstrating the role of *autoimmune mechanisms and the dysfunction of the basal ganglia.* In Sydenham's chorea antibodies against group A beta-hemolytic streptococcus cross-react with basal ganglia.

Monoclonal antibodies in patients who had SC that were targeted to *N-acetyl-beta-D-glucosamine,* the dominant epitope of GAS, showed specificity to mammalian lysoganglioside, a CNS ganglioside that influences neuronal signal transduction. Sera from these patients contained antibodies that targeted human neuronal cells and specifically induced calcium/calmodulin–dependent protein (CaM) kinase II activity (whereas sera from convalescing patients or from patients who had other streptococcal-related diseases lacked activation of this enzyme). Activation of CaM kinase II has been shown to cause increased release of *dopamine* in brain tissue, a mechanism by which clinical symptoms might ensue. Sera from patients who have SC also have been found to modify *intracellular calcium levels in PC12 cells* by a complement-independent mechanism. of patients who have SC correlated directly with the ELISA optical density values for ABAGs. (Teixeira, 2005) The binding of autoantibodies to these neuronal cell surface antigens may promote signal transduction, leading to the release of excitatory neurotransmitters and down regulation of several types of serotonergic neurons.

Pediatric Autoimmune Neuropsychiatric Disorders Associated With Streptococcal Infections ("Pandas")

OCD often presents itself in childhood and when it does so it is frequently co-morbid with tics and Tourette's syndrome. Precipitating streptococcal infection (GAS) in children with sudden onset of OCD symptoms but no chorea led to the coining of the term PANDAS (Pediatric Autoimmune Neuropsychiatric Disorders Associated with Streptococcus) by Giedd, and Rapoport and colleagues (1996) at the Child Psychiatry Branch of the National Institutes of Mental Health. This research group reported on a single case study of a male child with severe worsening of obsessive-compulsive symptoms following infection with group A beta-hemolytic streptococci. Giedd et al suggested that a pediatric autoimmune neuropsychiatric syndrome associated with streptococcal infections (PANDAS) may arise when antibodies directed against invading bacteria cross-react with basal ganglia structures, resulting in exacerbations of obsessive-compulsive disorder (OCD) or tic disorders..

Murphy, Goodman and colleagues (2002) suggested that untreated recurrences of streptococcal infection may result in more chronic presentations of OCD caused by unchecked autoantibody formation in brain tissue such as of the basal ganglia or frontal cortex. In 2004 Snider and Swedo published another article on PANDAS and proposed the strategy of continuous penicillin prophylaxis throughout childhood and adolescence in opposition to direct immune modulating treatments such as IVIG. The position of the NIMH researchers advocating antibiotic prophylaxis and opposing immune modulating treatments has been questioned by a variety of researchers (Arnold and Richter, 2001; Gimzal et al, 2002).

Dale et al (2005) examined 50 children with OCD for ABGA using enzyme-linked immunosorbent assay (ELISA) and western immunoblotting. The findings were compared with pediatric autoimmune (n=50), neurological (n=100) and streptococcal (n=40) controls. They found that the mean ABGA binding on ABGA binding on ELISA was elevated in the patient cohort compared with all control groups (P<0.005 in all comparisons). Western immunoblotting revealed positive antibody binding (as seen in Sydenham's chorea) in 42% of the patient cohort compared with 2-10% of control groups (P<0.001 in all comparisons).

Mell et al (2005) conducted a crucial study in children 4 to 13 years old receiving their first diagnosis of OCD or Tourette's Disorder (TD) between January 1992 and December 1999 (Group Health Cooperative outpatient facilities in California). They found patients with OCD or TD disorder were more likely than controls to have had prior streptococcal infection the 3 months before onset date. Importantly, the risk was higher among children with multiple streptococcal infections within 12 months. This fits with the proposed theory that multiple insults to the central nervous system can have an additive effect culminating in symptom expression.

IMMUNE SYSTEM, CYTOKINES, AND THE BRAIN

The immune system is considered to be a diffuse sensory organ and regulator of metabolism which works in concert with the nervous system to achieve and maintain homeostasis throughout the body. Immunocompetent cells are located throughout the body in virtually every organ – including the brain. Sophisticated and highly complex interactions that are both health enhancing and health detracting occur among these cells. In the main, these interactions are orchestrated by soluble protein messengers called cytokines of which there are many different varieties. Cytokines are produced in the brain during normal development and function, but are expressed at much higher levels in response to infection or damage. Influenza or bacterial infections such as *E. coli* can induce cytokine production even within the maternal immune system, the fetal immune system, and the placenta (Hillier et al, 1993) and certainly at later stages in human development (Hagberg and Mallard, 2005). Increased cytokine exposure during key periods of brain development may actually act as a vulnerability factor for later-life development of neuro-behavioral pathology by sensitizing the neuronal system (Bilbo and Schwarz, 2009).

The interactions between the cytokine-dominated immune and central nervous systems (CNS) in pathological states such as multiple sclerosis and depression have long been under investigation. Cytokines serve multiple functions in the central nervous system and play a central role in complex CNS functions including cognition (Rothwell and Hopkins, 1995; Pollmacher et al., 2002; Wilson et al., 2002). Indeed, the over-expression of cytokines has been associated with numerous pathological states within the central and peripheral nervous system, such as infection (viral, bacterial and fungal), autoimmune disease (i.e. multiple sclerosis), stroke, trauma, neurodegenerative disease (i.e. Alzheimer's disease (AD) and other dementias) (Rothwell and Loddick, 2002; Shaftel et al., 2008) and in neuropsychiatric disorders, such as depression (Capuron and Dantzer, 2003; Kronfol and Remick, 2000; Raison et al., 2006). Some cytokines, such as interleukin 1beta (IL-1-beta), interleukin 6 (IL-6) and tumor necrosis factor (TNF) have been associated with cognitive decline and dementia including Alzheimer's Disease (TNF and IL-1-beta) in several cross-sectional and prospective population studies (Dik et al., 2005).

Cytokine receptors are distributed throughout the brain with their highest concentrations are in the hippocampal region and basal ganglia, the latter of which – as indicated above - is implicated in the pathophysiology of OCD. Cytokines find their receptor match in microglias which are the primary immunocompetent cells of the brain. Microglias are present in every major aspect of brain development, function and disease. In response to injury or stimulation, microglia become considerably more active and up-regulate a number of surface receptors producing the cytokines which in turn influence neuronal function (Barres, 2008). While microglia serve helpful functions in the nervous system, excessive activation of the microglia is correlated with multiple neuroinflammatory and neurodegenerative disorders (e.g. Parkinson's, Multiple Sclerosis, Alzheimer's Disease, Huntington's Disease)

IMMUNE SYSTEM DYSFUNCTION IN OCD

Many pathophysiolgical processes including Syphilis, Lyme Disease, vascular disorders, tumors, and neurodegenerative disease processes such as Parkinson's Disease, post-streptococcal reactive arthritis (PSRA), Huntington's Chorea, Lupus and Multiple Sclerosis are all well-known to cause primary and, or secondary psychological sequalli. The phenomena of *anti-neuronal antibodies* was first observed in Sydenham's chorea (Husby, 1977). These antibodies recognized calls within the sub thalamic and caudate nuclei and were absorbed by streptococcal cellular components. (These findings are consistent with the concept of molecular mimicry - cross-reactivity between antigens in disease-associated streptococci and brain proteins.)

During the last few years, an increased interest in the possibility of *immune mediated pathophysiology of Obsessive Compulsive Disorder* and related disorders has emerged. Several lines of accumulating evidence support this theory. In 1994 Kiessling, Marcotte and Culpepper at Brown University conducted fluorescent serum antibody assessments of a group of children with OCD and their healthy controls. The sera from clinical cases showed antibodies directed against caudate, putamen, or both providing evidence of basal ganglia involvement in OCSD.

In the same year, Roy et al, at the VA Medical Center in Albany, New York reported on patients with Obsessive Compulsive Disorder (OCD) who demonstrated significant levels of antibody for somatostatin-28, its C-terminal fragment somatostatin-14, and prodynorphin - with contrasting lower levels of reactivity for somatostatin-28(1-14) (the N-terminal fragment of somatostatin-28) and negligible reactivity for several other peptides including beta-endorphin and corticotrophin. (Healthy volunteers and disease controls [schizophrenia, Alzheimer's disease, multiple sclerosis, and subjects with advanced human immunodeficiency virus (HIV) infection] exhibited negligible reactivity.) The researchers concluded that this reactivity raised the consideration of an autoimmune mechanism for some forms of OCD. Other early researchers (Black et al, 1998), however, reported an absence of correlation between markers of autoimmunity and OCD.

Sydenham's chorea is a choreaform disorder arising in the aftermath of Acute Rheumatic Fever (ARF) which in turn is triggered by group A beta-hemolytic streptococcal infections. As a late symptom of ARF, Sydenham's chorea usually occurs 3 months or longer after the streptococcal infection. In 1995 researchers at the National Institute of Mental Health (Allen et al, 1995) reported increased levels of obsessive compulsive symptoms in patients with Sydenham chorea (SC). Indeed, obsessive-compulsive symptoms occur in 70% of patients with Sydenham's chorea. The NIH group went on to suggest that in Sydenham's chorea antibodies against group A beta-hemolytic streptococcus may cross-react with basal ganglia neurons.

As a neuropsychiatric disorder Sydenham's chorea may present with emotional lability, anxiety, obsessive compulsive symptoms, attention deficit and hyperactivity symptoms or tics. Two main types of immunological changes have been described in patients with Sydenham's Chorea: (1) presence of anti-neuronal antibodies in serum CSK and (2) changes in host *B*-lymphocyte markers such as tumor necrosis factor alpha, a pro-inflammatory cytokine involved in several autoimmune diseases.

Monoclonal antibodies in SC patients targeted to N-acetyl-beta-D-glucosamine, the dominant epitope of GAS, have been identified. Sera from patients who have SC also have been found to modify intracellular calcium levels in PC12 cells by a complement-independent mechanism. The binding of autoantibodies to these neuronal cell surface antigens may promote signal transduction, leading to the release of excitatory neurotransmitters and down-regulation of several types of serotonergic neurons.

THE BLOOD-BRAIN BARRIER (BBB) AND ITS PERMEABILITY

The blood-brain barrier (BBB) is crucial to maintaining a precisely regulated microenvironment for reliable neuronal signaling among the highly excitable neurons and glial cells of the brain in part by regulating the influx and efflux of substances. Serving as the brain's protective shield it regulates soluble factors and cellular exchanges from blood to brain. Part of a network of capillaries supplying brain cells - the blood-brain barrier (BBB) is a separation of circulating blood and cerebrospinal fluid (CSF) maintained by the choroid plexus in the central nervous system (CNS). It is composed of highly dynamic brain microvascular endothelial cells (BMVEC), a collagen matrix, and astrocytes. The endothelial cells line cerebral microvessels characterized by the presence of tight junctions (high-density cells restricting passage of substances from the bloodstream much more than endothelial cells in capillaries elsewhere in the body) and relative lack of endocytic vesicles. The tight junctions are reinforced by the foot processes of the astrocytes (also known as "glia limitans") - which are composed of smaller subunits, frequently biochemical dimers, that are transmembrane proteins such as occludin, claudins, or junctional adhesion molecule for example. Each of these transmembrane proteins is anchored into the endothelial cells by another protein complex that includes zo-1 and associated proteins. As a unit the BBB restricts the diffusion of microscopic objects (e.g. bacteria) and large or hydrophilic molecules into the CSF, while allowing the diffusion of small hydrophobic molecules (O_2, hormones, CO_2). Cells of the barrier actively transport metabolic products such as glucose across the barrier with specific proteins.

A reduction in the competence of the BBB can lead to host proteins becoming recognizable to the immune system through molecular mimicry. The adhesion molecules and chemokine receptors provide attractive targets for neuroinflammatory diseases because of their important role in mediating central nervous system inflammation. Pathways thought to initiate BBB dysfunction include the kinin system, excitotoxicity, neutrophil recruitment, mitochondrial alterations and macrophage/microglial activation. All of these converge at the same nexus – reactive oxygen species.

On the other side of the BBB recent experiments indicate that the CNS itself may have an innate immune system comprised of astrocytes and microglia capable of regulating the initiation and progression of immune responses (Chaudhuri, 2000; Carson, 1999). Brain inflammation due to infection, hemorrhage, and aging is associated with activation of the local innate immune system as expressed by infiltrating cells, resident glial cells, and neurons. The innate immune response relies on the detection of ligands behaving by a plethora of pattern recognition receptors (PRRs) expressed by phagocytes to promote the clearance of pathogens, toxic cell debris (amyloid fibrils, aggregated synucleins, prions), and apoptotic cells accumulating within the brain parenchyma and the cerebrospinal fluid (CSF). These PRRs (e.g., complement, TLR, CD14, scavenger receptors) are highly conserved between vertebrates and invertebrates and may represent the most ancestrally innate scavenging system involved in tissue homeostasis. However, in some diseases, these protective mechanisms lead to neurodegeneration on the ground that several innate immune molecules have neurocytotoxic activities. This response represents a fine balance between protective and detrimental effects.

In addition, an accumulating body of evidence
demonstrates that the cellular components of the BBB are
themselves immunocompetent. Perivascular cells
(astrocytes, macrophages and microglial cells) and
BMVEC produce inflammatory factors that affect BBB
permeability and expression of adhesion molecules. These
affect cell trafficking into the CNS. (Leukocyte BBB
migration can be influenced by cytokines and chemokines
produced by glia.)

NEURONEUROIMMUNE MEDIATED OCD (NM-OCD)

It appears likely that a *cytokine-mediated pathophysiological processes* play a significant role in the cognitive impairments associated with a number of neuropsychiatric diseases. Cytokines, then, may make ideal targets for therapeutic intervention (Reichenberg et al., 2001; Tobinick, 2007; Wilson et al., 2002). Just as the nervous system is able to modulate immune activity, conversely, components of the immune system affect brain function. Cytokines are increasingly being recognized as mediators of such bidirectional communication. The exact schema of cytokine function within the CNS has yet to be determined and will likely involve a complex interplay between cytokines, their soluble and cell membrane receptors, and local factors related to neuronal activation and metabolism.

2001 Dinn et al (2001) reported on a series of chart reviews of adult OCD patients which revealed an increased rate of immune-related symptoms and syndromes in comparison to other anxiety and mood disorder groups. Groups did not differ significantly in the incidence of non-immune symptoms and syndromes. The researchers concluded that adult OCD patients appear to have an increased rate of immune-related diseases above and beyond that seen in other psychiatric disorders.

Guerrero and Hishinuma (2003) found that relative to other ethnicities, Native Hawaiians had a 2-fold higher risk for OCD and similarly higher rates of Sydenham's chorea. Degree of Polynesian ancestry correlated positively with OCD prevalence. The authors suggest that characteristics of OCD in this sample imply the need to consider the possibility of a streptococcal origin and the need for further studies to clarify the genetic and environmental risk factors for OCD in Hawaiian and other Polynesian youth.

Denys and Fluitman (2004) examined ex vivo production of TNF-alpha, IL-4, IL-6, IL-10, and IFN-gamma in whole blood cultures, and NK-cell activity and peripheral blood NK cell-, monocytes-, T-cell-, and B-cell-percentages were measured in 50 medication-free outpatients with OCD and 25 controls. In OCD patients the researchers found a significant decrease in production of TNF-alpha ($p < 0.0001$) and NK-activity ($p = 0.002$) in comparison with controls. (No significant differences were observed in the other immune variables.) Patients with first-degree relatives with OCD had significant lower NK-activity than patients who had no relatives with OCD ($p = 0.02$), and patients with a childhood onset of OCD had significantly lower number of NK-cells than patients with a late onset ($p= 0.003$). It was apparent that changes in TNF-alpha and NK activity pointed toward potential role of altered immune function in the pathophysiology of obsessive-compulsive disorder.

Kansy et al (2006) identified the M1 isoform of the glycolytic enzyme, pyruvate kinase (PK) as an autoimmune target in Tourette syndrome and associated disorders. Antibodies to PK reacted strongly with surface antigens of infectious strains of streptococcus, and antibodies to streptococcal M proteins reacted with PK. Moreover, immunoreactivity to PK in patients with exacerbated symptoms who had recently acquired a streptococcal infection was 7-fold higher compared to patients with exacerbated symptoms and no evidence of a streptococcal infection. These data suggest that PK can function as an autoimmune target and that this immunoreactivity may be associated with Tourette syndrome, OCD, and associated disorders – lending further support to the hypotheses that other immune destabilizing illnesses may result in anti-brain antibodies.

At the University of Florida in 2007 Murphy, and Goodman and colleagues conducted a broad review of the research in immune-mediated OCD. Among other conclusions they suggested that untreated reoccurrences of streptococcal infections may result in the more chronic presentations of OCD in adults caused by unchecked autoantibody formation to brain tissue such as of the basal ganglia or frontal cortex.

An interesting study by Bhattacharyya et al (2009) examined the role of the blood-brain barrier (BBB) in allowing autoantibodies to cross into the basal ganglia and how they might cause hyperactivity in the OCD circuit (the cortical-thalamic-striatal circuit). This group investigated the presence of autoantibodies directed against the basal ganglia (BG) or thalamus in the serum as well as CSF of 23 OCD patients compared with 23 matched psychiatrically normal controls. They also examined CSF amino acid (glutamate, GABA, taurine, and glycine) levels as well as the extent to which these levels were related to the presence of autoantibodies. There was evidence of significantly more binding of CSF autoantibodies to homogenate of BG as well as to homogenate of thalamus among OCD patients compared with controls. There was no significant difference in binding between patient and control sera except for a trend toward more bands to BG and thalamic protein corresponding to 43 kD among OCD patients compared with controls. CSF glutamate and glycine levels were also significantly higher in OCD patients compared with controls. Further multivariate analysis of variance showed that CSF glycine levels were higher in those OCD patients who had autoantibodies compared with those without.

Also, in 2009, Gause et al compared antibrain antibody profiles in children with OCD-only, OCD+PANDAS, OCD+Chronic Tic Disorder, and controls using ELISA (orbitofrontal (OFC) and dorsolateral prefrontal cortex (DLPFC), caudate (CD), cingulate gyrus (CG)), immunoblotting (four regions plus putative antigens), and immunohistochemistry. In their researches ELISA and immunohistochemistry showed no differences among groups. Immunoblot, however, showed that a greater percentage of individuals in the OCD+PANDAS cohort had reactive bands at 27 kDa (CD, CG, DLPFC), 36 kDa (CD), and 100 kDa (CD, OFC) and increased peak height at 67 kDa (all regions).

Giedd et al (2000) conducted a fascinating study in which they assessed selective basal ganglia involvement in a subgroup of children with obsessive-compulsive disorder (OCD) and/or tics believed to be associated with streptococcal infection. Using computer-assisted morphometric techniques, they analyzed the cerebral magnetic resonance images of 34 children with presumed streptococcus-associated OCD and/or tics and 82 healthy comparison children who were matched for age and sex. The average sizes of the caudate, putamen, and globus pallidus, but not of the thalamus or total cerebrum, were significantly greater in the group of children with streptococcus-associated OCD and/or tics than in the healthy children. The differences were similar to those found previously for subjects with Sydenham's chorea compared with normal subjects. These findings continued the consistent hypothesis of an autoimmune response to streptococcal infection.

In 2009 Maina and colleagues tested whether a group of 74 adults with OCD might have anti-brain antibodies or other antibodies that serve as markers of autoimmunity when compared to 44 controls with a current Major Depressive Episode for neurological symptoms. Testing ALSO titers, anti-tissue and anti-thyroid antibodies by immunohistochemistry and Western blotting methods the researchers found that the proportion of subjects with tic comorbidity or positive ASLO titer (>200 IU/ml) was significantly greater in OCD than in MDE patients (21.6 vs. 2.3% and 16.3 vs. 2.3%, respectively). No other differences in antibody parameters were found. Among OCD patients 5.4% (and none of the controls) were positive for anti-brain antibodies, with a band around 50-60 kDa at the Western blot analysis. A greater percentage of subjects with positive ASLO titers were found among OCD patients.

DIAGNOSTIC AND TREATMENT INNOVATIONS

*"Of course we don't know what we are doing. That is why
it is called research"*- Albert Einstein

A cautionary note is in order before proceeding
further into a discussion of some of the *potential and
possible* diagnostic and treatment options for NM-OCD.
None of these strategies have enough controlled research
behind them to warrant actual use by the public at this time.
That said, throughout history patients and their families
have debated the value of safety against the need for relief
from suffering. For some intrepid individuals one of the
ideas presented here might seem worth perusing on a
personal basis, given the alternative of great suffering when
other more mainstream measures have failed them. Over
this, as an author merely presenting data, I have no control.
I would strongly encourage keeping your physician and
other treating professionals informed of your intentions and
activities. They cannot stop you – only provide a backstop
should your efforts on your behalf go awry.

From the forgoing discussion it seems clear that
there are *three general levels* of activity or *"phases" in the
process of neuroimmunological compromise* in
Neuroimmune Mediated Obsessive Compulsive Disorder.
The first is the *Autoimmune Phase* in which the immune
system begins the cascade of events leading to antibrain
antibody formation. The second is the *Blood-brain barrier
Phase* in which there is a "failure" of the BBB to screen
access by errant elements of the immune system to the
brain and prevent the introduction of these elements into

the CNS. Finally, in the *Brain Phase* the brain has already been infiltrated and the question becomes how to remediate unwanted antineuronal effects.

In medicine appropriate treatment proceeds from the least invasive and safest intervention options to those that are more invasive and carry greater risk. In the case of OCSD this forces us to engage in pragmatic reasoning on the molecular or at least neuronal level. For example, it might appear that prevention of PANDAS through use of prophalacitc antibiotics is low on the scale of invasiveness / risk the potential negative alterations in the very immunologic systems which are problematic may actually make this a highly invasive and risk-prone option. Thus, in the case of OCSD treatment, interventions which which rely upon behavioral changes or on the introduction of substances which the body recognizes as being of a natural biologic origin will be those that carry the lowest level of risk / invasiveness.

An example of a low invasive / risk intervention might be ingestion of an antioxidant such as ginkolide B or Cognitive Behavioral Therapy. Moving up the scale of risk we might arrive at enzymatic or cytokine-modifying substances and eventually reach psychotropic medications and finally ablative neurosurgery. On behalf of our patients who are the ultimate recipients of our researches, the principle of least invasive and lowest risk must always guide us – though this sometimes will put us at odds with tradition.

With this in mind our discussion, will now proceed
in reverse order beginning with the more standard lines of
intervention which at this time appear to carry greater
practical risk/invasiveness. (Interestingly these lines of
intervention tend to approach the brain directly. Medicine
has often been criticized for treating the symptom at the
end of a chain of physiologic events rather than the
originating cause. Certainly in the case of
psychopharmacological interventions this appears to have
been the case up until very recently.)

We will necessarily be confining our investigations
to Obsessive Compulsive Disorder alone as the specifics of
treatment methodology differs too widely for some of the
other Obsessive Compulsive Spectrum Disorders and space
does not permit such a wide ranging exposition. (It's is
likely, however, that the principles underlying many of
these treatment options share overlap between some of the
OCSD.)

Autoimmune Phase Interventions

Antioxidants play an important role in remediating
the effects of reactive oxygen species (ROS) which are
implicated in many neurodegenerative diseases. Oxidative
damage has been known to be involved in flammatory and
auto-immune tissue destruction in which modulation of
oxygen free-radical production represents a new approach
to the treatment of inflammatory and autoimmune diseases
(Gilgun-Sherki and Melamed, 2003). Mitochondria-
targeted antioxidants and antioxidant "cocktails" combined
with other drugs enabling them to pass through biological

membranes such the Blood-brain barrier are in development. In 2007 Murphy and Smith reported on a conjugated formulation of lipophilic triphenylphosphonium cation to an antioxidant moiety such as **ubiquinol** or **alpha-tocopherol**. Commonly encountered antioxidants include **Vitamins C, E and A (or mixed carotenes), dihydrolipoate, alpha-lipoate,** and **glutathione.** Because alpha-lipoate can be directly administered it may be useful in many neurogenerative disorders. (Packer et al, 1997)

Flavonoids, an amazing array of over 6,000 different substances, are found in virtually all plants. The chemistry of flavonoids is complicated, and within the non-technical term "flavonoids" can be found many different chemical groups of substances. These groups include flavonols, dihydroflavonols, flavones, isoflavones, flavanones, anthocyanins, and anthocyanidins. Within each of these groups fall hundreds, and sometimes thousands of different flavonoids. Well-known flavonols include **quercetin, rutin, and hesperidin**, while well-known flavones include **apigenin and luteolin.** (Many of these substances such as rutin appear to have activity only outside the Blood-brain barrier and not within the brain.) Flavonoids are often named directly after the unique plant that contains them. **Ginkgetin** is a flavonoid from the ginkgo tree, and **tangeretin** is a flavonoid from the tangerine.

While the flavonoid family is too complex to report all of its food connections, some highlights are especially important. In the fruit family, it is berries that come out highest in the chemical category of flavonoids called anthocyanins. ***Black raspberries***, for example, may contain up to 100 milligrams of anthocyanins per ounce. Virtually all fruits, vegetables, herbs and spices contain flavonoids. They are also found in other types of food, including dry beans (where they give red beans, black beans, and speckled beans their color) and grains (where the color provided by flavonoids is usually in the yellow family). Products made from the foods above (for example, wines made from grapes) also typically contain a wide variety of flavonoids.

Green tea has flavonoid components called catechins that may reach 1,000 milligrams (or 1 gram) per cup. In general the more colorful components of the food - like the skins of fruits - contain the highest concentration of flavonoids. An exception to this rule, however, is the white pulpy inside of ***oranges***. Unlike the watery orange-colored sections of this fruit, which contain virtually all of its vitamin C, the orange's flavonoids are found in the white pulpy portion inside the skin and surrounding the sections.

Many types of cells involved with the immune system - including T cells, B cells, NK cells, mast cells, and neutrophils - have been shown to alter their behavior in the presence of flavonoids. Prevention of *excessive inflammation* appears to be a key role played by many different chemical categories of flavonoids. In some cases, flavonoids can act directly as antibiotics by disrupting the function of microorganisms like viruses or bacteria. The antiviral function of flavonoids has been demonstrated with the HIV virus, and also with HSV-1, a herpes simplex virus. Flavonoids can protect the brain by their ability to modulate intracellular signals promoting cellular survival. Epidemiological studies have shown beneficial effects of flavonoids on several of the neurodegenerative disorders. Quercitin in particular has received a great deal of research attention, but appears to require the addition a preparation (e.g. *lecithin/quercitin*) to the blood-brain barrier. Dajas et al (2003) suggest that a group of quercitin-related flavonoids could become lead molecules for the development of neuroprotective compounds with multitarget anti-ischemic effects – however other studies suggest that quercitin may in some circumstances have reactive oxygen and mutogenic effects of its own and should be approached with more caution than other antioxidant flavonoids.

Most flavonoids function in the human body as antioxidants. In this capacity, they help neutralize overly reactive oxygen-containing molecules and prevent these overly reactive molecules from damaging parts of cells. *Scultellaria root, cornus fruit, licorice*, and *green tea* are examples of flavonoid-containing foods widely used in oriental medicine. While flavonoids may exert their cell structure protection through a variety of mechanisms, one of their potent effects may be through their ability to *increase levels of glutathione*, a powerful antioxidant, as suggested by various research studies.

While most human consumption of flavonoids is through *fruits and vegitables*, common supplemental form of flavonoids are the citrus flavonoids quercetin, rutin, and hesperidin. Of these three, the most common is quercetin. Doses in commonly sold supplements usually range from

25-200 milligrams, although clinical studies using flavonoids often use much higher level interventions in the 500-3,000 milligram range. It is not difficult to reach the 1,000-milligram range from dietary intake, if the diet contains an adequate amount of whole, properly prepared fruits and vegetables. Even in very high amounts (for example, 140 grams per day), flavonoids do not appear to cause unwanted side effects. Even when raised to the level of 10% of total caloric intake, flavonoid supplementation has been shown non-toxic. Studies during pregnancy have also failed to show problems with high-level intake of flavonoids.

However, heat, degree of acidity (pH), and degree of processing can have a dramatic impact on the flavonoid content of food. For example, in fresh cut spinach, boiling extracts 50% of the total flavonoid content. With onions (a less delicate food), boiling still removes about 30% of the flavonoids (and specifically, a group of flavonoids called the quercitin glycosides). Overcooking of vegetables has particularly problematic effects on this category of nutrients. Additionally, poor intake of fruits and vegetables - or routine intake of high-processed fruits and vegetables - are common contributing factors to flavonoid deficiency. It is difficult to overemphasize the impact of processing and a non-whole foods diet on flavonoid intake. If the pulpy, fibrous parts of fruits are eliminated from the juice, and the vibrant natural colors of canned vegetables are lost during repeated heating, risk of flavonoid deficiency is greatly increased. Finally, research has clearly documented the synergistic (mutually beneficial) relationship between flavonoids and vitamin C. Each substance improves the antioxidant activity of the other, and many of the vitamin-related functions of vitamin C also appear to require the presence of flavonoids.

Food polyphenols such as curcumin, resveratrol and catechins have been employed in the treatment of several neurodegenerative diseases and have been shown to have brain protective activities. (Rossi et al, 2008)

Plasma DHEA shows a progressive age-related decline in men and women. *DHEA and Androstenedione* have been shown to inhibit IL-6 secretion from human mononuclear cells in vitro, providing a tantalizing connection between endocrine senescence and immunosenescence. DHEA has been shown to suppress peripheral IL-4, IFN and astrocytic TNF and IL-6 production and thus may possess central antinflammatory properties. Despite its interesting inverse association with IL-6 levels and purported beneficial effects on senescence and cognition, a recent Cochrane Systematic Review found only limited evidence of an improved sense of well-being with DHEA and no evidence that short-term DHEA administration produced cognitive improvement.

Agomelatine, a potent agonist at type 1 and 2 melatonin receptors, selectively inhibits serotonin.

TNF and IL-1 production have been shown to be inhibited after dietary supplementation with *fish oils containing 20- and 22-carbon n-3 fatty acids*. Whether dietary modulation can influence brain-associated cytokine dysregulation is unclear, but bears close scrutiny by researchers.

Montelukast sodium (MS) is marketed under the product name Singulair for the treatment of allergic rhinitis and asthma. Montelukast sodium is a selective and orally active leukotriene receptor antagonist that inhibits the cysteinyl leukotriene CysLT1 receptor. The cysteinyl leukotrienes (LTC4, LTD4, LTE4) are products of arachidonic acid metabolism and are released from various cells, including mast cells and eosinophils. These eicosanoids bind to cysteinyl leukotriene (CysLT) receptors. The CysLT type-1 (CysLT1) receptor is found in smooth muscle cells and on other pro-inflammatory cells (including eosinophils and certain myeloid stem cells). (Leukotriene-mediated effects include airway edema, smooth muscle contraction, and altered cellular activity associated with the inflammatory process.) Administration of MS has been shown to decrese total eosinophil count in peripheral venous blood, serum IL-13, and IFN-gamma levels and stimulate improvement rates for IgE, total eosinophil, IL-13, and IFN-gamma levels   LPS-induced SDF-1 expression and SDF-1-induced chemotaxis of monocytic (THP-1) cells and decrease serum and sputum levels of eosinophil cationic protein and IL-8 and sputum levels of myeloperoxidase, and increased serum and sputum levels of IL-10. Montelukast treatment results in a significant decrease of eosinophils in the nasal mucosa, and in either bone marrow interleukin (IL)-5-, but not IL-3-, or granulocyte-macrophage colony-stimulating factor-responsive eosinophil/basophil colony-forming units, and

IL-5-stimulated eosinophil maturation. These results indicate that cysLT1-R antagonism in vivo limits both IL-5-responsive eosinophilopoiesis, acting at several stages of eosinophil differentiation and maturation. The anti-allergic effects of cysLT1-R antagonists are consistent with the concept that cysLTs and IL-5 act together in the recruitment of eosinophils and eosinophil progenitors from the marrow during the human inflammatory process. (saito et al, 2004; Stelmach et al, 2005; Hung et al, 2007)

Caloric restriction models have suppressed age-associated increases in GFAP, a marker of reactive astrogliosis, and in corpus callosal TGF-1. Thus, at least in aging rats, caloric restriction holds some promise as a means of delaying general neurodegeneration. Whether this would have an implication of OCSD is unclear, but the temporal association is intriguing.

The positive effects of ***aerobic exercise*** on psychological well-being are well known. Aerobic exercise also seems to contribute to improvements in cognitive performance. Long-term exercise programs (as opposed to acute exercise training) have been associated with reductions in peripheral cytokine levels. For example, a 6-month exercise program in patients with multiple cardiac risk factors led to reductions in peripheral mononuclear cell production of IFN, IL-1, and TNF. Exercise training shifts cytokine production to a more antiinflammatory profile, it is possible that exercise-induced adjustments in peripheral cytokines are responsible for the beneficial psychological and cognitive effects of exercise.

Blood-brain barrier Phase

Although mentioned during the discussion of the *Inflammatory Phase*, antioxidants appear to play a role in all three "phases" of neroimmune dysfunction. Reactive oxygen species are known to mediate the transendothelial migration of monocytes and induce a dysfunction of the blood-brain barrier. *Alpha-lipoic acid (LA)* appears to have a beneficial effect on this process by reducing the migratory capacity of monocytes and also by stabilizing the BBB (Schreibelt et al, 2006)

Melatonin is an indoleamine hormone endogenously produced in the pineal gland and in other organs. It has been found to act as a protective agent following brain trauma (Maldonado, 2007). Melatonin crosses the Blood-brain barrier with the ability to stabilize celluar membranes preventing vasospasm and apoptosis of endothelial cells. Melatonin also has well-known chonobiological effects acting to rest the natural circadian rhytum of sleep and wakefulness. (Reiter et al, 2007).

Ginkgolide B crosses the Blood-brain barrier in a concentration dependent manner and exerts a protective effect in various regions of the brain and possibly on the BBB in the process. (Fang et al, 2009) The standardized Ginkgo Biloba extract EG761 appears to have direct protective effects on mitochondria. EG761 protects against the decrease of cytochrome c oxidase (COX) activity, mitochondrial ATP content and mitochondrial glutathione (GSH) content in both platelets and hippocampi (Shi et al, 2009)

In very promising studies emerging from cardiology research Angiotensin II (AT2) receptors have been identified within the neurons of the blood-brain barrier confirming the existence of an endogenous brain Angiotensin II system responding to ATII generated in and, or transported into the brain. Well-defined actions of AT2 in the brain include regulation of hormone formation and release, control of the central and peripheral sympathoadrenal system and regulation of water and sodium intake. Antagonistic blockade of brain AT1 receptors using drugs such as *angiotensin II type 1 (AT1) receptor antagonists, immunosuppressive agents or HMG-CoA reductase inhibitors (statins)* could be considered as a novel therapeutic approach to inflammation in the brain and normalization of the sympathoadrenal systems. Indeed Saavedra (2005) reported that AT1 antagonistic blockade completely prevented the hormonal symathoadrenal response.

Some general information regarding this class of medications may be helpful. Several new antiarrhythmic drugs are on the cusp of introduction into clinical practice. *Vernakalant* affects several atrially expressed ion channels and has rapid unbinding Na+-channel blocking action along with promising efficacy for AF conversion to SR. *Dronedarone* is an amiodarone derivative with an electrophysiological profile similar to its predecessor but lacking most amiodarone-associated adverse effects. Drugs emerging or in use in atrial fibrillation treatment include those that block atrial-selective ion-channel targets such as the ultra-rapid delayed rectifier current (IKur) and the acetylcholine-regulated K+-current (IKACh) are presently in development. Flecainide, propafenone, quinidine, and sotalol are equally effective in preventing recurrences of AF. Amiodarone has been demonstrated to be more efficacious than propafenone or sotalol in the Canadian Trial of Atrial Fibrillation. In persistent AF, twice-daily dofetilide has been shown to be as or more effective than low-dose sotalol given twice daily for the maintenance of sinus rhythm in patients with AF. Trials have demonstrated that subjective adverse effects are less frequent with class IC drugs, sotalol, and dofetilide compared with such drugs as quinidine. In patients without structural heart disease, flecainide, propafenone, and D,L-sotalol are the initial drugs of choice, given their reasonable efficacy, low incidence of subjective side effects, and lack of significant end-organ toxicity. Neutral effects on survival and favorable hemodynamics have positioned amiodarone and dofetilide as the antiarrhythmics of choice in patients with left ventricular dysfunction. In post-myocardial infarction patients, sotalol is an additional agent to consider for treatment of AF in this setting.

Glucocoticoids (GL) are being evaluated for use in restoring the vascular barrier properties of the retina, rebalancing the matrix metalloproteinases and their endogenous inhibitors the TIMPs (tissue inhibitors of metalloproteinases). GL is used in preserving the integrity of the BBB in the treatment of brain tumors. Glucocorticoids may act by both suppressing inflammation and by directly affecting the endothelial cells by regulating phosphorylation. (Felinski and Antonetti, 2005; Hartman et al, 2009)   Hydrocortisone in particular selectively upregulates TIMP-3 while TIMP-1, TIMP-2 and TIMP-4 are downregulated on the mRNA-level. Further research will likely advance our abilities to use GL in restoring the blood-brain barrier in a number of neuropsychological diseases.

Elevated lipid levels are found more frequently in the serum of OCD patients.   Advances in Alzheimer Disease (AD) research suggest that ***central nervous system lipids*** play a key role in the pathogenesis. These seemingly unrelated findings may be attributable to the high lipid content of CNS structures and the presence of the blood-brain barrier which disables the exchange of lipids between plasma and CNS. Cholesterol is a unique molecule in the CNS. Special apolipoproteins used for the recycling of cholesterol within the CNS and special brain-specific oxysterols contribute to the uniqueness of CNS cholesterol. Now suspected to be protective in AD, there is promise for some statin drugs to have a beneficial impact on monocytes infiltration and BBB permeability. Experiments with ***lovastatin***,   a   immunomodulatory   3-hydroxy-3methylglutaryl coenzyme A reductase inhibitor, reduced both cerebrovascular leakage and monocytic trafficking. (Floris at al, 2004; Sagin and Sozmen, 2008)

Early pregancy factor (EPF) is a secreted protein with immunosuppressive and growth factor properties that has been shown to to suppress or down-regulate the cell-mediated inflammatory response and adhesion molecule expression and thereby remediate acute experimental autoimmune encephalomyelitis. Recombinant rEPF treatment reduces the numbers of lymphocytes and macrophages in the CNS, possibly through an effect on cellular communication. (Athanasas-Platsis et al, 2003; Zhang et al, 2003)

Growth hormone (GH) and insulin-like Growth Factor I (IGF-I) receptors are expressed in many brain areas including hippocampus, pituitary and hypothalamus. GH (secreted during slow-wave sleep) and IGF-I can pass the BBB by an as yet incompletely understood mechanism and can also be produced within the brain itself. An improvement in cognitive function in GH-deficient patients by GH substitution has been shown. The role of GH and IGF-I in OCD has yet to be determined, but the ability of these molecules to pass the BBB raises questions that they may play a role in psychneuroimmunologic pathogenesis.

In recent years *bilibrubin* has been demonstrated to have a potent antioxidant effect in vitro. Bilirubin can interfere with the invasion of inflammatory cells into the central nervous system by protecting the Blood-brain barrier from free radical induced permeability changes. However, in some cases inflammation still occurred even though no clinical illness was observed. (Liu et al, 2003)

Several novel agents, compounds and processes (for example the delicate *balance between pro- and anti-inflammatory cytokines* and how this is maintained) may eventually provide clues to remediating the Blood-brain barrier permeability in neurodynamic diseases such as OCD.

In a few recent studies, it has been shown that the BBB expresses two types of ATP-binding cassette (ABC) transporters - the multidrug transporters *P-glycoprotein (P-gp)* and the multidrug resistance-related protein 1 (MRP1). *MRP1* potentially contributes to detoxification of the brain, as a whole, as it is also expressed at the level of the BBB. P-gp, however, while also functioning as an efflux pump at the BBB, has an opposite transport direction at the level of the BBB – toward the CSF. P-gp may therefore raise the concentration of neurotoxic P-gp substrates in the CSF.

Treatment of mice induced with viral encephalomyelitis using the *anti-CXCR2 blocking antibody* reduced migration of cytokines into the CNS by 95%. (Hosking et al, 2009) These findings highlight a previously unappreciated role for ELR-positive chemokines in enhancing hots defense during viral infection against the CNS.

In different experimental models of CNS injury, *growth hormone IGF-I* has been found to increase progenitor cell proliferation and new neurons.

Blood-brain barrier permeability to cytokines and other unwanted invaders does not confer the same level of access to helpful molecules. *Nanotechnology* may eventually be of assistance in the transfer of healing drugs across the BBB – or, more importantly for our purposes, in repairing the functioning of the BBB. Recently, researchers have been trying to build liposomes loaded with nanoparticles to gain access through the BBB. More research is needed to determine which strategies will be most effective and how they can be improved.

Another possibility is to invent antioxidants that are selectively accumulated into the mitochondria within patients. These compounds could pass more easily through all biological membranes including the BBB.

Aquaporin-4 (*AQP4*) is the primary cellular water channel in the brain, localized to astrocytic foot processes along the blood-brain barrier and brain-cerebrospinal fluid interfece. Drug therapy targeting AQP4 function and expression may dramatically alter our ablility to treat cerebral edema and other events beyond the BBB. (Bloch and Manley, 2007)

Researchers have found several *glial proteins* in the central nervous system that have promise as protective agents in the treatment of neurodegenerative disease. (Brenneman et al, 2000) *SR 57746A* is a nonpeptide drug without classical immunosuppressive properties which has been shown to efficiently protect the BBB and impared intrathecal IgG synthesis and consequently suppresses signs of autoimmune encephalomyelitis.

Several key regulatory mechanisms have been evidenced in the control of CNS innate immunity and could be harnessed to explore novel therapeutic avenues – in particular *neuroregulatory proteins or NIRegs* (e.g. CD95L, TNF, CD200, CD47, CD55, CD46, C3a HMGB1, fh, sialic acids) which have direct beneficial effects on neurogenesis, contribute to brain tissue remodeling and are involved in the silencing of innate immunite at the cellular and molecular levels and supressino of inflammation. Griffith et al (2007) found that NIRegs played an important role in controlling lymphocyte/macrophage/microglia hyperinflammatory responses while sparing host defense and repair mechanisms.

Hypothermia has long been known to be a potent neuroprotectant and is in use in the treatment of stroke and ischemia. Hypothermia protects brain tissue by retarding energy depletion, reducing intracellular acidosis, and lessening the ischemic overdose of excitatory neurotransmitters. (Hammer and Krieger, 2003)

NXY-059 is a polar compound with limited transport across the BBB has demonstrated neuroprotection. A clinically attainable concentration of 250 mumol/L of NXY-059 administered at the onset or up to 4 hours after oxygen glucose deprivaton (OGB) produced a significant reduction in the increased BBB permeability caused by OGD. The researchers concluded tha the neuroprotective effects of NXY-059 may be attributable to its ability to restore functionality of the brain endothelium.

The novel potent and selective PDE IV inhibitor *mesopram* has shown immunomodulatory activity. Mesopram selectively inhibits the activity of type 1 helper T cells without affecting cytokine production or proliferation of type 2 helper T cells.

Some researchers believe that the cytokinregulated *Jak/SAT* intracellular signaling pathway may hold some eventual contributions to BBB dysfunction. (Chitnis and Khoury, 2003)

Unlike malignant tissues, neuronal cells have to be protected, but only if the protection does not disturb natural cell elimination. Defining molecular mechanisms it, therefore, a necessary step preceding the adaptation of new protective and then, possibly, therapeutic strategies. At present the most promising are discoveries related to *caspases, JNK, and GSK-3beta* and their crucial role in stress-dependent and spontaneous apoptosis (cell death). These substances coss the blood-brain barrier easily and exert profound neuroprotective action. (Kajta, 2004)

There is now a vast and emerging literature on processes and substances which can have a beneficial impact on blood-brain barrier permeability. To prevent infiltration by cytokines and other unwanted molecules into the brain microenvironment would be to eliminate the neuroimmune mediation in Obsessive Compulsive Spectrum Disorders.

Brain Phase

Several key regulatory mechanisms have now been evidenced in the control of the innate immunity within the brain itself. Of particular importance are neuroimmune regulatory proteins (NIRegs), such as CD95L, TNF, CD200, CD47, sialic acids, CD55, CD46, fH, C3a, HMGB1, which are involved in silencing innate immunity at the cellular and molecular levels and suppression of inflammation. For instance, NIRegs may play an important role in controlling lymphocyte/macrophage/microglia hyperinflammatory responses, while sparing host defense and repair mechanisms. Moreover, NIRegs have direct beneficial effects on neurogenesis and contributing to brain tissue remodeling. In addition to the NIRegs, tumor necrosis factor alpha, interferon-gamma, interleukin-6, pro-inflammatory cytokines (discussed previously in this monograph) may yield clues to NM-OCSD treatment.

Utilizing the PANDAS concept Perlmutter et al (1999) theorized that if post-streptococcal autoimmunity is the cause of the symptom exacerbations pediatric patients might respond to *immunomodulatory treatments such as plasma exchange or intravenous immunoglobulin (IVIG)*. In a very small study they examined whether plasma exchange or IVIG would be better than placebo (sham IVIG) in reducing severity of neuropsychiatric symptoms. Thirty children entered the study and 29 completed the trial. Ten received plasma exchange, nine IVIG, and ten placebo. At 1 month, the IVIG and plasma exchange groups showed striking improvements in obsessive-compulsive symptoms (mean improvement on children's Yale-Brown obsessive compulsive scale score of 12 [45%] and 13 [58%], respectively), anxiety (2.1 [31%] and 3.0 [47%] improvement on National Institute of Mental Health anxiety scale), and overall functioning (2.9 [33%] and 2.8 [35%] improvement on National Institute of Mental Health global scale). Tic symptoms were also significantly improved by plasma exchange (mean change on Tourette syndrome unified rating scale of 49%). Treatment gains were maintained at 1 year, with 14 (82%) of 17 children "much" or "very much" improved over baseline (seven of eight for plasma exchange, seven of nine for IVIG).

In 2003 Swedo and Snider (2003) reporting on a placebo-controlled trial, revealed that both intravenous immunoglobulin and plasma exchange were effective in reducing neuropsychiatric symptom severity (40 and 55% reductions, respectively) for a group of severely ill children in the "PANDAS" subgroup. They then recommended that these procedures should not be used by physicians treating children with "PANDAS".

As discussed in both previous *Phases*, both experimental and clinical studies have demonstrated that *antioxidants* can play a surprisingly significant role in NM-OCSD treatment. *Melatonin* is a neurohormone synthesized and secreted by the pineal gland. *Edaravone (3-methyl-1-phenyl-2-pyrazolin-5-one)* is a newly developed synthetic drug. Both substances have shown an ability to cross the blood-brain barrier and ameliorate oxidative stress in the brain and providing a neuroprotective effect. Edaravone has been shown to reduce oxidative stress, edema, infarct volume, inflammation and apoptosis following ischemic injury of the brain as well as decrease free radical production in the neonatal brain following hypoxic-ischemic insult. Kaur and Ling, 2008).

Selenium has been intensively investigated as an antioxidant trace element. It is widely distributed throughout the body, but is particularly well maintained in the brain, even upon prolonged dietary selenium deficiency.

Several selenoproteins are expressed in the brain, but many questions remain about their roles in neuronal function. *Slenoprotein P* has been repoted to posess antioxidant activities and the ability to promote neuronal cell survival.

Experimental findings support the use of *recombinant human growth factor erythropoietin (rh-EPO)* in human brain disease including acute ischemic stroke, chronic schizophrenia and chronic progressive multiple sclerosis. rhEPO appears to be a viable neuroprotective/neuroregenerative treatment option in neuropsychiatric disease and may have applicability to MN-OCSD (Siren et al, 2009)

Transcranial magnetic stimulation (TMS) was introduced as a neurophysiological technique in 1985 when Anthony Barker and his team developed a compact machine that permitted non-invasive stimulation of the cerebral cortex (Barker, 1985). Since its introduction, TMS has been used to evaluate the motor system, to study the function of several cerebral regions, and for the pathophysiology of several neuropsychiatric illnesses. In addition, more recently a form of TMS has been approved by the USFDA for therapeutic use including in depression.. Some controlled studies have evaluated the effects of *repetitive Transcranial Magnetic Stimulation (rTMS)* in patients with obsessive-compulsive disorder (OCD). There is evidence that motor and premotor cortex are hyperexcitable in obsessive-compulsive disorder (OCD) and Tourette's syndrome (TS). Greenberg (1997) observed that a single session of right prefrontal cortex stimulation produced a significant decrease in compulsive urges in OCD patients lasting over eight hours. In a recent study subjects with OCD or TS were treated with active rTMS to the supplementary motor area (SMA) for 10 daily sessions at 1 Hz, 100% of motor threshold, 1200 stimuli/day. Suggestions of clinical improvement were apparent as early as the first week of rTMS. At the second week of treatment, statistically significant reductions were seen in the YBOCS, YGTSS, CGI, HARS, HDRS, SAD, BDI, SCL-90, and SASS. Symptoms improvement was correlated with a significant increase of the right resting motor threshold and was stable at 3 months follow-up. Slow rTMS to SMA resulted in a significant clinical improvement and a normalization of the right hemisphere hyperexcitability, thereby restoring hemispheric symmetry in motor threshold (Gross et al, 2007). Whether neuroimmune processes mediated these improvements has yet to be determined, other studies have had negative findings and there are methodological problems inherent with rTMS research. It is, however, clear at this point rTMS warrants continued investigation by researchers concerned with OCSD treatment.

Assuming inflammatory cytokines play a role in Immune Mediated OCSD then *cytokine antagonists* developed for other purposes such as treating cognitive decline, dementia, autoimmune disease or other neuropsychiatric disorders may play a role in the remediation of NM-OCSD. An increasing number of cytokine modifying drugs are coming online. Intracerebroventricular administration of *IL-1ra* in rodents, for example, prevents memory deficits following the psychological stress of social isolation (Pugh et al. 1999), and intracerebroventricularly administered antibodies to TNF-a have antidepressant effects in the forced swim test (Reynolds et al. 2004). In humans, administration of TNF-alpha blockers such as *etanercept* (Enbrel1; Amgen, USA) and *infliximab* (Remicade1; Johnson and Johnson, USA) have been found to attenuate depressive symptoms that accompany immune system activation in psoriasis (Dantzer, 1999; Krishnan et al. 2007; Tyring et al. 2006; Yirmiya, 2000). In addition, inhibition of the production of pro-inflammatory cytokines, such TNF-a and IL-1 by *celexocib* induced a rapid antidepressant response and prevented cognitive decline in patients with MDD and BPD (Muller et al. 2006; Nery et al. 2008). Similarly, the anti-inflammatory drugs of this class can both inhibit inflammation-induced increases in pro-inflammatory cytokines and oppose their effects in the central nervous system (CNS). *Etanercept*, a TNF-receptor antagonist, is of particular interest in that it has been explored for use in the treatment of rheumatoid arthritis – a close model for NM-OCSD. Recipients of anticytokine therapies such as etanercept often claim an improved sense of wellbeing. Reduction in inflammation by TNF, in theory, might preserve cognition in neurodegenerative disorders. Because it has been shown that imbalance between pro-and anti-inflammatory cytokines might be involved in the pathogenesis of depressive disorders it is possible that *anti-inflammatory cytokines such as IL-4 and IL-10* which have a rather broad spectrum of action may also be useful anti-cytokine therapies. Although more in-depth cognitive assessment is required in future studies of such subjects, if confirmed, Etanercept might become a treatment adjunct for OCSD.

Other potential anti-cytokine strategies include *cytokine synthesis inhibitors, soluble cytokine receptors, antibodies against cytokine receptors*, and other novel cytokine receptor antagonists. Systemic postinjury administration of IL-1ra attenuates regional cell death and cognitive dysfunction after experimental brain injury in rats. However, IL-1 knockout mice manifest detrimental effects such as impaired host response to mycobacterial infection and impaired production of the regenerative mediator and ciliary neurotropic factor after CNS trauma; thus additional studies in animal models are required before further consideration of IL-1ra as a therapeutic agent.

Considerable interest surrounds the potential neuroprotective properties of *estrogen* and *progesterone* against excitotoxic, oxidative, or Ab peptide–induced insult. Estrogen administration has been shown to improve verbal memory on cognitive testing and limit the degree of ischemic injury from stroke in humans. Many of these proposed beneficial effects are thought to involve cytokines. Various estrogens have been found to inhibit production of IL-1 from human peripheral monocytes, suppress expression of IL-1 and IL-6 in vascular smooth muscle cells, suppress TNF and IFN gene expression, and

activate anti-inflammatory microglial pathways. In AD
models, estradiol has been shown to decrease the Ab
peptide and LPS-induced activation of NF and to attenuate
the IL-1 response to Ab peptide. In addition, estrogen has
been shown to enhance clearance of Ab peptide by
microglia.

Progesterone is produced in the brain, for the brain,
by neurons and glial cells in the central and peripheral
nervous system. There is evidence that the hormone
affords protection from several forms of actue CNS injury
including penetrating brain trauma, stroke, anoxic brain
injury, and spinal cord injury. Progesterone appear to exert
it's protective effects by defending and, or rebuilding the
Blood-brain barrier, decreasing development of cerebral
edema, down-regulating the inflammatory casdace, and
limiting cellular necrosis and apoptosis. (Stein et al, 2008)

Depression is commonly associated with
hypercortisolemia and glucocorticoid resistance. This might
imply that the raised levels of inflammatory cytokines seen
in depression are related to a failure of *glucocorticoid-
mediated feedback* leading to elevated cortisol, subsequent
glucocorticoid resistance and a decrease in glucocorticoid-
mediated immunosuppression. Indeed, recent analysis
revealed that the raised cytokines cause the glucocorticoid
resistance by impairing the function of glucocorticoid
receptors. Thus, glucocorticoid resistance might constitute
further evidence that failure of immunoregulation is a
primary factor in the effects of drugs used to treat
depression. More tenuous evidence that the increased
serum cytokines might be contributing to vulnerability to

depression (rather than merely a consequence of depression) comes from the observation that antidepressant drugs modulate cytokine production in vitro. It has been suggested that all antidepressants reduce the *IFN-g:IL-10 ratio*, and so exert an overall anti-inflammatory effect. Therefore, there might be relevant peripheral as well as CNS targets of these drugs.

The development of new neurochemical probes that explore the sensitivity of various *5HT receptor subtypes* has provided precious brain-mapping information – providing more specific information as to just how serotonergic neurotransmission occurs in OCSD. The orbitofrontal cortex (OCD), caudate (OCD), medial pre-frontal/cingulate (OCD, SAD, PTSD), temporal (OCD, SAD, PTSD) and, thalamic regions (OCD, SAD) are some of those implicated. *m-Chlorophenylpyperazine* (m-CPP), an agonist to 5HT1A, 5HT1D, and 5HT2C receptors, which also blocks 5HT3 receptors, exacerbates OC symptoms. Additionally, the 5HT1D receptor appears to be aggravated in response to *sumatriptan*, a selective 5HT1D receptor agonist. In contrast, neither *MK-212 (6-chloro-2-[1-piperazinyl]-pyrazine)*, a 5HT1A and 5HT2C receptor agonist, nor *ipsapirone* or *buspirone*, which acts as an agonist to 5HT1A receptors, have any effect on OC symptom severity. It appears then that 5HT3 plays no specific role, given the lack of influence of the 5HT3 antagonist ondansetron, on OC symptom intensity.

When drugs affecting serotonin function (e.g., tryptophan, fenfluramine, lithium, buspirone) are added to SRI therapy in SRI-refractory patients, results are mixed and not consistently encouraging. However, when *drugs affecting dopamine function (e.g., pimozide, haloperidol, risperidone)* are added to SRI therapy in SRI-refractory OCD patients, individuals with either a personal history or family history of tics experience a reduction in their symptoms

Tryptophan, added to the *SRI-pindolol regimen*, produced a significant improvement after 4 weeks, with further amelioration after 6 weeks (36% decrease of the Yale-Brown Obsessive Compulsive Score), which was maintained with treatment prolongation. In another study addition of the 5-HT1A 1 beta-adrenergic antagonist pindolol did not alter OCD symptomatology but produced a rapid improvement of depressive symptoms. The 5-HT1A agonist buspirone as well as 5-hydroxytryptophan, the immediate precursor of 5-HT, added to the SRI-pindolol regimen, were not effective in attenuating the intensity of OCD.

The addition of drugs that enhance serotonin (5-HT) neurotransmission, such as **lithium** and **buspirone**, to ongoing treatment in SUI-refractory patients has generally proved to be an ineffective strategy. The addition of dopamine antagonists to the regimens of SUI-resistant patients appears to be a useful approach for OCD patients

An augmentation study of *risperidone* (acting on different neurotransmitter systems) demonstrated response in a putative OCD subsample (e.g. 4/9) of patients, identifying that low metabolic rates in the striatum and high metabolic rates in the anterior cingulum predicted improvement (Buchsbaum et al 2006). *Neuroleptics,* unfortunately, are generally associated with high degrees of toxicity.

Hyperbaric oxygen therapy (H-ox) has significant neuroprotective effects and is being examined for possible additional clinical uses. H-ox leads to the activation of ion channels, inhibition of hypoxia inducible factor 1-alpha, upregulation of Bcl-2, inhibition of MMP-9, decreased cyclooxygenase-2 activity. Decreased myeloperoxidase activity, up-regulation of superoxide dismutase and inhibition of Nogo-A growth inhibiting factor. (Matchett et al, 2009)

Cymbalta has sometimes shown itself to be useful in monotherapy with OCD patients. Reports indicate reduced sexual side effects with this drug option.

Citalopram treatment (in very high doses – 160 mg/day) resulted in significant deactivation of various serononergically dominated areas of the brainincluding superior and anterior cingulate, right thalamus and left hippocampus. Deactivation within the left precentral, right mid-frontal, right inferior frontal, left prefrontal and right precuneus was more marked in treatment responders.

Comparisons between *buspirone* and the *benzodiazepines* in treating patients with generalised anxiety disorder with the reference standards; in those patients with OCD, there are only preliminary indications of efficacy, which merit a more adjunctive role.

*Adding   agents   that   enhance   5-HT
neurotransmission* to ongoing treatment in patients whose
OCD is refractory to 5-HT reuptake inhibitors has not
yielded impressive results. However, the addition *of low-
dose dopamine (DA) antagonists* to the regimens of
treatment-resistant patients appears to be a potentially
useful strategy for the specific subgroup of OCD patients
with a comorbid chronic tic disorder such as Tourette's
syndrome. These drug response data suggest that both the
5-HT and dopamine systems may be involved in the
treatment, and possibly the pathophysiology, of specific
subtypes of OCD.

Augmenting strategies reported to decrease OCD
severity in randomized controlled trials to date include
atypical antipsychotics *risperidone* (Li et al 2005),
quetiapine (Denys et al 2004) and *olanzapine* (Bystritsky
et al 2004), which act on serotonergic-dopaminergic
systems. Open-label studies and reports have also
supported use of *trazodone* (Goodman et al 1993; Marazziti
et al 1999), *aripiprazole* (Connor et al 2005), *topiramate*
(Hollander and Dell'Osso 2006; Van Ameringen et al
2006), and *mirtazapine* (Koran et al 2005; Pallanti et al
2004).

Some of the most promising psychopharmacologic
agents now being explored in OCD treatment are the
glutamatergic agents. These agents includ *riluzole* (Coric
et al 2005), *n-acetylcysteine* (Lafleur et al 2006) and
memantine (Hezel et al 2009). To date only a handful of
controlled studies of glutamatergic augmenting agents have
yet been reported in OCD. *Riluzole* is primarily an

inhibitor of glutamate release but also inactivates voltage-
dependent sodium channels in cortical neurons and blocks
GABA reuptake. Riluzole has shown promise for
ameliorating the symptoms of OCD. Riluzole is well
tolerated and is Food and Drug Administration approved
for treatment of amyotrophic lateral sclerosis.84Y86. More
recently, an open-label trial in children (8Y16 years) with
OCD found riluzole to be beneficial and well tolerated.90
A larger placebo-controlled trial at NIMH is under way.
Memantine (Namenda) is a glutamate receptor antagonist
that has been reported to reduce OCD symptoms in case
studies of treatment-resistant individuals (Pasquini &
Biondi, 2006; Poyurovsky, Weizman, Weizman, & Koran,
2005). This medication was FDA approved in 2003 and
appears to be safe with few reported side effects and no
reported serious or lethal side effects. There are no known
cardiotoxic or hepatotoxic effects. It is not associated with
tolerance or withdrawal and is not metabolized by the
CP450 cytochrome system, thus increasing its ease of use
in combination with other medications. Use of this
medication for management in OCD would be considered
'off label' at present, and it has not been approved
specifically for use in children, which is a valid
consideration given that OCD frequently onsets in
childhood. However, a recent case report of its safe use in
adolescence has been published (Hezel et al 2009).

DISCUSSION AND GENERAL RECOMMENDATIONS

The high rate of OCD symptoms in SC has prompted exploration of autoimmune involvement in OCD and other OC Spectrum Disorders. Studies such as those discussed above are now suggesting a neuroimmunological component in at least a significant subgroup of pediatric *and* adult OCD patients. Although further investigations are needed to demonstrate its etiopathogenetic relevance, it is clear that for a meaningful percentage of OCD patients autoimmune reactions towards neuronal structures are present. There is now sufficient evidence to revise the limiting PANDAS terminology, broaden it to *Neuroimmune Mediated Obsessive Compulsive Disorder (NM-OCD)*. This new nomenclature of MN-OCD will provide a platform for contemporary researchers to pursue: (1) prospective studies to identify infectious triggers in the onset and exacerbations of OCD spectrum disorders, (2) biological measures for immune and genetic susceptibility, and (3) large scale epidemiological studies demonstrating the relationship between infection and OCD spectrum disorders.

(1) The grouping of Obsessive Compulsive Spectrum Disorders (OCSD) are linked to one degree or another by both shared diagnostic and biological and treatment characteristics.

(2) There is a connection between immune events and OCD symptom perturbation in many patients. This connection is probably not limited to OCD and can be seen in several of the OCSD.

(3) Attempts to study and provide working treatments for NM-OCSD have been hampered by a too limited definition the situation including a focus on one age group and one type of immune event (streptococcal infections).

(4) NM-OCSD should be viewed as having at least three levels of cascading effects beginning with the *NeuroImmune Phase* – continuing across a compromised *Blood-Brain-Barrier Phase (BBB)* – and culminating in anti-neuronal antibodies in a susceptible *Brain Phase*. Research and interventional strategies may be directed at any of these points and at their convergences.

(5) It is essential that the blood-brain barrier (BBB) should be a major target for research in NM-OCSD as it is in other fields of brain pathology. Existing findings on BBB pathology should be integrated into the emerging body of NM-OCSD research.

(6) Approaching NM-OCSD as a three-part process allows us to examine treatments at all three levels of immune system, BBB, and brain. Very importantly this broadened focus will lead to incorporation of treatment strategies emerging in other fields. (For example several of the diabetic drugs appear to have some utility in slowing the progression of Multiple Sclerosis via a strengthening of the BBB.) Treatments which strengthen the ability of the Blood-brain barrier to prevent neural contamination resulting in antineuronal antibodies should be aggressively sought.

(7) NM-OCSD may occur at any age (with children, aged and immune compromised persons likely being at greater risk), in a gradient between acute and chronic, be seminal or contributory, be bi-directional, and be triggered by many types of viral and bacterial immune events,

(8) Immune events comprise only one part of the complex picture of OCD and it may be greater or lesser in different patients and diagnostic groups.

(9) Genetic determinants for the various OCSD have been emerging. Research should be directed to determine if genes involved in immune response might be disrupted in OCSD patients. (e.g. the myelin oligodendrocyte glycoprotein (MOG) gene)

A FINAL COMMENTARY

Researchers, particularly in the healthcare area, provide spectacular information through their efforts – information that is too seldom seen or utilized by practitioners. As a result, there is an unacceptably wide gulf between research and practice in many areas of medicine. This is definitely the case with Obsessive Compulsive Spectrum Disorders, leading to unnecessary patient suffering. It is our contention and challenge to researchers and those who direct research that an additional section be added to all juried research articles for *Treatment or Practice Recommendations*. It is our contention that it should be review policy for controlled research articles in the applied medical and behavioral fields that each article with potential application to human welfare *include no less than 3 actionable treatment recommendations* at the conclusion of the paper (not to include the recommendation for "further research"). The adoption of this simple formatting change could lead the saving of untold lives and the resolution of wide swaths of human suffering.

REFERENCES

Albert U, Maina G, Bogetto F, Chiarle A, Mataix-Cols D.
Clinical predictors of health-related quality of life in
obsessive-compulsive disorder. Compr Psychiatry. 2010
Mar-Apr;51(2):193-200. Epub 2009 Apr 16.

Allen AJ, Leonard HL, Swedo SE. Case study: a new
infection-triggered, autoimmune subtype of pediatric OCD
and Tourette's syndrome. *J Am Acad Child Adolesc
Psychiatry 1995;34*(3):307–11.

Arnold P. D and Richter M. A. Is obsessive–compulsive
disorder an autoimmune disease? *Can. Med. Assoc. J.*
2001; 165: 1353-1358

Athanasas-Platsis S, Zhang B, Hillyard NC, Cavanagh AC,
Csurhes PA, Morton H, McCombe PA. (2003). Early
pregnancy factor suppresses the infiltration of lymphocytes
and macrophages in the spinal cord of rats during
experimental autoimmune encephalomyelitis but has no
effect on apoptosis. *J Neurol Sci.* Oct 15;214(1-2):27-36.

Avital A, Goshen I, Kamsler A, Segal M, Iverfeldt K,
Richter-Levin G, Yirmiya R (2003). Impaired interleukin-1
signaling is associated with deficits in hippocampal
memory processes and neural plasticity. *Hippocampus* 13,
826–834.

Barker AT, Jalinous R, Freeston IL. Non-invasive magnetic
stimulation of human motor
cortex. *Lancet* 1985;(8437):1106–1107

Barres B. A. (2008). The Mystery and Magic of Glia: A
Perspective on Their Roles in Health and Disease.
Neuron, Volume 60, Issue 3, 430-440.

Beattie EC, Stellwagen D, Morishita W, Bresnahan JC, Ha BK, Von Zastrow M, Beattie MS, Malenka RC. Control of synaptic strength by glial TNFalpha. *Science.* 2002;295:2282–2285.

Bhattacharyya , S., Khanna, S. , Chakrabarty, K., Mahadevan , A., Christopher, R., & Shankar, S. K. (2009). Anti-Brain Autoantibodies and Altered Excitatory Neurotransmitters in Obsessive|[ndash]|Compulsive Disorder. *Neuropsychopharmacology* 34, 2489–2496

Bilbo SD, Schwarz JM. (2009) Early-life programming of later-life brain and behavior: a critical role for the immune system. *Front Behav Neurosci.* 3:14.

Black JL, Lamke GT, Walikonis JE. (1998). Serologic survey of adult patients with obsessive-compulsive disorder for neuron-specific and other autoantibodies. *Psychiatry Res.* Dec 14;81(3):371-80.

Bloch O, Manley GT.(2007). The role of aquaporin-4 in cerebral water transport and edema. *Neurosurg Focus.* 2007 May 15;22(5)

Bolton J, Moore GJ, MacMillan S, Stewart CM, Rosenberg DR. Case study: caudate glutamatergic changes with paroxetine persist after medication discontinuation in pediatric OCD.
J Am Acad Child Adolesc Psychiatry. 2001 Aug;40(8):903-6.

Brenneman, D.E., et al.; "Protective Peptides Derived from Novel Glial Proteins;" 2000; Biochemical Society Transactions; vol. 28; Part 4; pp. 452-455.

Buchsbaum MS, Hollander E, Pallanti S, Baldini Rossi N, Platholi J, Newmark R, et al (2006): Positron emission tomography imaging of risperidone augmentation in serotonin reuptake inhibitor-refractory patients. *Neuropsychobiology* 53:157-168.

Bystritsky A, Ackerman DL, Rosen RM, Vapnik T, Gorbis E, Maidment KM, et al (2004): Augmentation of serotonin reuptake inhibitors in refractory obsessive-compulsive disorder using adjunctive olanzapine: a placebo-controlled trial. *The Journal of clinical psychiatry* 65:565-568.

Capuron, L., Dantzer, R., 2003. Cytokines and depression: the need for a new paradigm. *Brain Behav. Immun.* 17 (Suppl. 1), S119–S124.

Carlsson ML. On the role of prefrontal cortex glutamate for the antithetical phenomenology of obsessive compulsive disorder and attention deficit hyperactivity disorder. *Prog Neuropsychopharmacol Biol Psychiatry.* 2001 Jan;25(1):5-26.

Carpenter LL, Heninger GR, McDougle CJ, Tyrka AR, Epperson CN, Price LH. Cerebrospinal fluid interleukin-6 in obsessive–compulsive disorder and trichotillomania. *Psychiatry Res* 2002;112:257–62.

Carson, M. J., Reilly, C. R., Sutcliffe, J. G. & Lo, D. (1999). Disproportionate recruitment of CD8+ T cells into the central nervous system by professional antigen-presenting cells. *American Journal of Pathology* 154, 481±494.

Chakrabarty K, Bhattacharyya S, Christopher R, Khanna S (2005): Glutamatergic dysfunction in OCD. *Neuropsychopharmacology* 30:1735-1740.

Chaudhuri, A., Behan, P.O., 2000. Fatigue and basal ganglia. *J. Neurol. Sci.* 179, 34–42.

Chitnis T, Khoury SJ. (2003). Cytokine shifts and tolerance in experimental autoimmune encephalomyelitis. *Immunol Res* 28(3):223-39.

Choi JS, et al. 2006. Morphometric alterations of anterior superior temporal cortex in obsessive-compulsive disorder. *Depress Anxiety* 23:290-6.

Connor KM, Payne VM, Gadde KM, Zhang W, Davidson JR: The use of aripiprazole in obsessive-compulsive disorder: preliminary observations in 8 patients. J Clin Psychiatry 66(1): 49-51, 2005.

Coric V, Taskiran S, Pittenger C, Wasylink S, Mathalon DH, Valentine G, et al (2005): Riluzole augmentation in treatment-resistant obsessive-compulsive disorder: an open-label trial. *Biol Psychiatry* 58:424-428.

Dajas F, et al, Neuroprotection by flavonoids. Braz J Med Biol Res. 2003 Dec;36(12):1613-20.

Dale RC, Heyman I, Giovannoni G, Church AJ. Incidence of anti-brain antibodies in children with obsessive–compulsive disorder. *Br J Psychiatry* 2005;187:314–9.

Dantzer R (1999). Mechanisms of the behavioral effects of cytokines. In: *Cytokines, Stress and Depression*. New York: Kluwer Academic/Plenum Publishers.

Denys D, de Geus F, van Megen HJ, Westenberg HG (2004): A double-blind, randomized, placebo-controlled trial of quetiapine addition in patients with obsessive-compulsive disorder refractory to serotonin reuptake inhibitors. *The Journal of clinical psychiatry* 65:1040-1048.

Denys D, Fluitman S, Kavelaars A, Heijnen K,Westenberg H. Decreased TNF-a and NK activity in obsessive–compulsive disorder. *Psychoneuroendocrinology* 2004;29:945–52.

Dickel et al. Association Testing of the Positional and Functional Candidate Gene *SLC1A1/EAAC1* in Early-Onset Obsessive-compulsive Disorder*Arch Gen Psychiatry*. 2006;63:778-785.

Dik, M.G., Jonker, C., et al., 2005. Serum inflammatory proteins and cognitive decline in older persons. *Neurology* 64 (8), 1371–1377.

DinnWM, Harris CL, McGonigal KM, et al. Obsessive-compulsive disorder and immunocompetence. *Int J Psychiatry Med* 2001;31(3):311–20. 466 MURPHY et al.

Felinski EA, Antonetti DA (2005) Glucocorticoid regulation of endothelial cell tight junction gene expression: novel treatments for diabetic retinopathy. Curr Eye Res 30:949–957
Floris S, Blezer EL, Schreibelt G, Döpp E, van der Pol SM, Schadee-Eestermans IL, Nicolay K, Dijkstra CD, de Vries HE. (2004) Blood-brain barrier permeability and monocyte

infiltration in experimental allergic encephalomyelitis: a quantitative MRI study. *Brain.* Mar;127(Pt 3):616-27.

Franklin ME and Foa EB. (2011) Treatment of obsessive compulsive disorder
Annu Rev Clin Psychol. 2011; (7):229-43.

Gabbay V, Coffey BJ, Guttman LE, Gottlieb L, Katz Y, Babb JS, Hamamoto MM, Gonzalez CJ. A cytokine study in children and adolescents with Tourette's disorder. Prog Neuropsychopharmacol Biol Psychiatry. 2009 Aug 31;33(6):967-71.

Gause C, Morris C, Vernekar S, Pardo-Villamizar C, Grados MA, Singer HS. Anti-neuronal antibodies in OCD: comparisons in children with OCD-only, OCD+chronic tics and OCD+PANDAS. J Neuroimmunol. 2009 Sep 29;214(1-2):118-24.

Giedd JN, Rapoport JL, Garvey MA, Perlmutter S, Swedo SE. MRI assessment of children with obsessive–compulsive disorder or tics associated with streptococcal infection. *Am J Psychiatry* 2000;157:281–3.

Giedd JN, Rapoport JL, Leonard HL, Richter D, Swedo SE. Case study: acute basal ganglia enlargement and obsessive–compulsive symptoms in an adolescent boy. *J Am Acad Child Adolesc Psychiatry* 1996;35:913–5.

Gilgun-Sherki Y, Melamed E, Offen D. Antioxidant
treatment in Alzheimer's disease: current state. J Mol
Neurosci. 2003;21(1):1-11.

Gimzal A, Topçuoğlu V, Yazgan MY. Acute rheumatic
fever, Sydenham's chorea and psychopathology. Turk
Psikiyatri Derg. 2002 Summer;13(2):137-41.

Giulino L, Gammon P, SullivanK, et al. Is parental report
of upper respiratory infection at the onset of obsessive-
compulsive disorder suggestive of pediatric autoimmune
neuropsychiatric disorder associated with streptococcal
infection? *J Child Adolesc Psychopharmacol
2002*;12(2):157–64.

Goodman WK, McDougle CJ, Barr LC, Aronson SC, Price
LH (1993): Biological approaches to treatment-resistant
obsessive compulsive disorder. *The Journal of clinical
psychiatry* 54 Suppl:16-26.

Goodman WK, Murphy TK, Storch EA. Risk of adverse
behavioral effects with pediatric use of
antidepressants.Psychopharmacology (Berl). 2007
Mar;191(1):87-96.

Goshen I, Kreisel T, Ounallah-Saad H, Renbaum
P, Zalzstein Y, Ben-Hur T, Levy-Lahad E, Yirmiya R. A
dual role for interleukin-1 in hippocampal-dependent
memory processes. Psychoneuroendocrinology. 2007 Sep-
Nov;32(8-10):1106-15.

Goshen I, Kreisel T, Ben-Menachem-Zidon O, Licht
T, Weidenfeld J, Ben-Hur T, Yirmiya R. Brain interleukin-
1 mediates chronic stress-induced depression in mice via

adrenocortical activation and hippocampal neurogenesis suppression. Mol Psychiatry. 2008 Jul;13(7):717-28.

Gross M, Nakamura L, Pascual-Leone A, Fregni F. Has repetitive transcranial magnetic stimulation (rTMS) treatment for depression improved? A systematic review and meta-analysis comparing the recent vs. the earlier rTMS studies. *Acta Psychiatr Scand.* 2007 Sep;116(3):165-73.

Guerrero AP, Hishinuma ES, Andrade NN, Bell CK, Kurahara DK, Lee TG, Turner H, Andrus J, Yuen NY, Stokes AJ. Demographic and clinical characteristics of adolescents in Hawaii with obsessive-compulsive disorder. Arch Pediatr Adolesc Med. 2003 Jul;157(7):665-70.

Hagberg H, Mallard C. Effect of inflammation on central nervous system development and vulnerability. Curr Opin Neurol. 2005 Apr;18(2):117-23.

Hammer MD, Krieger DW. Hypothermia for acute ischemic stroke: not just another neuroprotectant. Neurologist. 2003 Nov;9(6):280-9.

Hartmann C, El-Gindi J, Lohmann C, Lischper M, Zeni P, Galla HJ. (2009). TIMP-3: a novel target for glucocorticoid signaling at the blood-brain barrier. *Biochem Biophys Res Commun.* Dec 11;390(2):182-6.

Hezel DM, Beattie K, Stewart SE (2009): Memantine as an Augmenting Agent for Severe Pediatric OCD. *Am J Psychiatry* 166:237.

Hillier SC, Godbey PS, Hanger CC, Graham JA, Presson RG Jr, Okada O, Linehan JH, Dawson CA, Wagner WW Jr. Direct measurement of pulmonary microvascular distensibility. J Appl Physiol. 1993 Nov;75(5):2106-11.

Hoexter, MQ, et al. (2009) The drug-naïve OCD patients imaging genetics, cognitive and treatment respons study: methods and sample description. Rev Bras PsiquiaTR. 2009 (31): 349-53.

Hoekstra PJ, Minderaa RB. Tic disorders and obsessive-compulsive disorder: is autoimmunity involved? Int Rev Psychiatry. 2005 Dec;17(6):497-502.

Hollander E, Dell'Osso B (2006): Topiramate plus paroxetine in treatment-resistant obsessive-compulsive disorder. *International clinical psychopharmacology* 21:189-191.

Hung CH, Jong YJ, Hua YM, Li CY, Lai YS, Yang KD, Chang HC. Regulation of stromal cell-derived factor-1 and exhaled nitric oxide in asthmatic children following montelukast and ketotifen treatment. *Pulm Pharmacol Ther.* 2007;20(3):233-9. Epub 2006 Apr 20.

Husby G, v de Rijn I, Zabriskie JB, Ardin ZH, Williams RC Jr. (1977) Anti-neuronal antibody in Sydenham's chorea. *Lancet.* 4;1(8023):1208.

Hutto JH, Ayoub EM. Cytotoxicity of lymphocytes from patients with rheumatic carditis in vitro. In: Read SE, Zabriskie JB, editors. *Streptococcal diseases and the immune response.* New York: Academic Press; 1987. p. 733–8.

Kansy JW, Katsovich L, McIver KS, Pick J, Zabriskie JB, Lombroso PJ, Leckman JF, Bibb JA. Identification of pyruvate kinase as an antigen associated with Tourette syndrome. J Neuroimmunol. 2006 Dec;181(1-2):165-76.

Kajta M. Apoptosis in the central nervous system: Mechanisms and protective strategies. Pol J Pharmacol. 2004 Nov-Dec;56(6):689-700.

Kaur C, Foulds WS, Ling EA. Hypoxia-ischemia and retinal ganglion cell damage. Clin Ophthalmol. 2008 Dec;2(4):879-89.

Kiessling LS, Marcotte AC, Culpepper L. Anti-neuronal antibodies: tics and obsessive-compulsive symptoms. *J Dev Behav Pediatr* 1994;15(6):421–5.

Koldzic-Zivanovic N, Tu H, Juelich TL, Rady PL, Tyring SK, Hudnall SD, Smith EM, Hughes TK. Regulation of adrenal glucocorticoid synthesis by interleukin-10: a preponderance of IL-10 receptor in the adrenal zona fasciculata. Brain Behav Immun. 2006 Sep;20(5):460-8. Epub 2005 Oct 25.

Koran LM, Gamel NN, Choung HW, Smith EH, Aboujaoude EN (2005): Mirtazapine for obsessive-compulsive disorder: an open trial followed by double-blind discontinuation. *The Journal of clinical psychiatry* 66:515-520.

Krishnan R, Cella D, Leonardi C, Papp K, Gottlieb AB, Dunn M, Chiou CF, Patel V, Jahreis A (2007). Effects of etanercept therapy on fatigue and symptoms of depression in subjects treated for moderate to severe plaque psoriasis for up to 96 weeks. *British Journal of Dermatology* 157, 1275–1277.

Kronfol, Z., Remick, D.G., 2000. Cytokines and the brain: implications for clinical psychiatry. *Am. J. Psychiatry* 157 (5), 683–694.

Lafleur DL, Pittenger C, Kelmendi B, Gardner T, Wasylink S, Malison RT, et al (2006): N-acetylcysteine augmentation in serotonin reuptake inhibitor refractory obsessive-compulsive disorder. *Psychopharmacology* (Berl) 184:254-256.

Lazaro L, et al. Brain changes in children and adolescents with obsessive-compulsive disorder before and after treatment: a voxel-based morphometric MRI study. 2009(2): 140-146.

Li X, May RS, Tolbert LC, Jackson WT, Flournoy JM, Baxter LR (2005): Risperidone and haloperidol augmentation of serotonin reuptake inhibitors in refractory obsessive-compulsive disorder: a crossover study. *The Journal of clinical psychiatry* 66:736-743.

Libby S, *Reynolds S*, Derisley J, Clark S. Cognitive appraisals in young people with obsessive-compulsive disorder. J Child Psychol Psychiatry. 2004 Sep;45(6):1076-84.

Liu Y, Zhu B, Wang X, Luo L, Li P, Paty DW, Cynader MS, (2003) Bilirubin as a potent antioxidant suppresses experimental autoimmune encephalomyelitis: implications for the role of oxidative stress in the development of multiple sclerosis. *J Neuroimmunol*. 2003 Jun;139(1-2):27-35.

Lougee L, Perlmutter SJ, Nicolson R, et al. Psychiatric disorders in first-degree relatives of children with pediatric autoimmune neuropsychiatric disorders associated with streptococcal infections (PANDAS). *J Am Acad Child Adolesc Psychiatry* 2000;39(9):1120–6.

Marazziti D, Gemignani A, Dell'osso L (1999): Trazodone Augmentation in OCD: A Case Series Report. *CNS spectrums* 4:48-49.

Marazziti D, Presta S, Pfanner C, Gemignani A, Rossi A, Sbrana S, et al. Immunological alterations in adult obsessive–compulsive disorder. *Biol Psychiatry* 1999;46:810–4.

Mell LK, Davis RL, Owens D. Association between streptococcal infection and obsessivecompulsive disorder, Tourette's syndrome, and tic disorder. *Pediatrics* 2005;116(1):56–60.

Miguel EC, Stein MC, Rauch SL, et al. Obsessive-compulsive disorder in patients with multiple sclerosis. *J Neuropsychiatry Clin Neurosci* 1995;7(4):507–10.

Murphy ML, Pichichero ME. Prospective identification and treatment of children with pediatric autoimmune neuropsychiatric disorder associated with group A streptococcal infection (PANDAS). *Arch Pediatr Adolesc Med* 2002;156(4):356–61.

Murphy T, Goodman W. Genetics of childhood disorders: XXXIV. Autoimmune disorders, part 7: D8/17 reactivity as an immunological marker of susceptibility to neuropsychiatric disorders. *J Am Acad Child Adolesc Psychiatry* 2002;41(1):98–100.

Nery FC, Zeng J, Niland BP, Hewett J, Farley J, Irimia D, Li Y, Wiche G, Sonnenberg A, Breakefield XO. TorsinA binds the KASH domain of nesprins and participates in linkage between nuclear envelope and cytoskeleton. J Cell Sci. 2008 Oct 15;121(Pt 20):3476-86.

Pallanti S, Quercioli L, Bruscoli M (2004): Response acceleration with mirtazapine augmentation of citalopram in obsessive-compulsive disorder patients without comorbid depression: a pilot study. *The Journal of clinical psychiatry* 65:1394-1399.

Pasquini M, Biondi M, Costantini A, Cairoli F, Ferrarese G, Picardi A, Sternberg C. Detection and treatment of depressive and anxiety disorders among cancer patients: feasibility and preliminary findings from a liaison service in an oncology division. Depress Anxiety. 2006;23(7):441-8.

Perlmutter SJ, Leitman SF, Garvey MA, et al. Therapeutic plasma exchange and intravenous immunoglobulin for obsessive-compulsive disorder and tic disorders in childhood. *Lancet* 1999;354(9185):1153–8.

Pollmacher T, Haack M, Schuld A, Reichenberg A, Yirmiya R (2002). Low levels of circulating inflammatory cytokines – do they affect human brain functions? *Brain, Behavior, and Immunity* 16, 525–532.

Raison, C.L., Capuron, L., Miller, A.H., 2006. Cytokines sing the blues: inflammation and the pathogenesis of depression. *Trends Immunol.* 27, 24–31.

Reichenberg A, Yirmiya R, Schuld A, Kraus T, Haack M, Morag A, Pollmächer T. Cytokine-associated emotional and cognitive disturbances in humans. Arch Gen Psychiatry. 2001 May;58(5):445-52.

Reiter RJ, Tan DX, Manchester LC, Tamura H. Melatonin defeats neurally-derived free radicals and reduces the associated neuromorphological and neurobehavioral damage. J Physiol Pharmacol. 2007 Dec;58 Suppl 6:5-22.

Rosenberg DR, Arnold PD, Mundo E, Tharmalingam S, Kennedy JL, Richter MA. Association of a glutamate (NMDA) subunit receptor gene (GRIN2B) with obsessive-compulsive disorder: a preliminary study. Psychopharmacology (Berl). 2004 Aug;174(4):530-8.

Rossi D Alpa M, Ferrero B, Cavallo R, Naretto C, Menegatti E, Di Simone D, Napoli F, La Grotta R, , Baldovino S, Sena LM, Roccatello D. Anti-neuronal antibodies in patients with HCV-related mixed cryoglobulinemia. Autoimmun Rev. 2008 Oct;8(1):56-8. Epub 2008 Aug 12.

Rothwell, N.J., Hopkins, S.J., 1995. Cytokines and the nervous system. II. Actions and mechanisms of action. *Trends Neurosci.* 18 (3), 130–136.

Rothwell, N.J., Loddick, S. (Eds.), 2002. *Immune and Inflammatory Responses in the Nervous System.Molecular and Cellular Neurobiology Series.* Oxford University Press, New York.

Roy M, Kiremidjian-Schumacher L, Wishe HI, Cohen MW, Stotzky G. Supplementation with selenium and human immune cell functions. II. Effect on cytotoxic lymphocytes and natural killer cells. *Biol Trace Elem Res*. 1994 Apr-May;41(1-2):115-27.

Roy M, Kiremidjian-Schumacher L, Wishe HI, Cohen MW, Stotzky G. Supplementation with selenium and human immune cell functions. II. Effect on cytotoxic lymphocytes and natural killer cells. Erratum in: Biol Trace Elem Res 1994 Oct-Nov;46(1-2):183.

Sagin FG, Sozmen EY. Lipids as key players in Alzheimer disease: alterations in metabolism and genetics. Curr Alzheimer Res. 2008 Feb;5(1):4-14.

Saito H, Morikawa H, Howie K, Crawford L, Baatjes AJ, Denburg E, Cyr MM, Denburg JA. Effects of a cysteinyl leukotriene receptor antagonist on eosinophil recruitment in experimental allergic rhinitis. *Immunology*. 2004 oct;113(2):246-52.

Saavedra JA. Hypertension in children and adolescents. Rev Port Cardiol. 2005 Sep;24(9):1091-4.

Schreibelt G, Musters RJ, Reijerkerk A, de Groot LR, van der Pol SM, Hendrikx EM, Döpp ED, Dijkstra CD, Drukarch B, de Vries HE. (2006) Lipoic acid affects cellular migration into the central nervous system and stabilizes blood-brain barrier integrity. *J Immunol*. Aug 15;177(4):2630-7.

Shaftel SS, Griffin WS, O'Banion MK. The role of interleukin-1 in neuroinflammation and Alzheimer disease: an evolving perspective. J Neuroinflammation. 2008 Feb 26;5:7.

Shi C, Fang L, Yew DT, Yao Z, Xu J. (2009). Ginkgo biloba extract EGb761 protects against mitochondrial dysfunction in platelets and hippocampi in ovariectomized rats. *Platelets.* 2009 Nov 25.

Sirén AL. Byts N, Erythropoietin: a multimodal neuroprotective agent. Exp Transl Stroke Med. 2009 Oct 21;1:4.

Slattery MJ, Dubbert BK, Allen AJ, et al. Prevalence of obsessive-compulsive disorder in patients with systemic lupus erythematosus. *J Clin Psychiatry* 2004;65(3):301–6.

Snider LA, Swedo SE. Post-streptococcal autoimmune disorders of the central nervous system. *Curr Opin Neurol* 2003;16:359–65.

Snider LA, Swedo SE. PANDAS: current status and directions for research. Mol   Psychiatry. 2004 Oct;9(10):900-7.

Stellwagen D, Malenka RC. Synaptic scaling mediated by glial TNF-alpha. Nature. 2006 Apr 20;440(7087):1054-9.

Stelmach I, Korzeniewska A, Stelmach W, Majak P, Grzelewski T, Jerzynska J. Effects of montelukast treatment on clinical and inflammatory variables in patients with cystic fibrosis. *Ann Allergy Asthma Immunol.* 2005 Oct;95(4):372-80.

Storch EA, Murphy TK, Geffken GR, Mann G, Adkins J, Merlo LJ, Duke D, Munson M, Swaine Z, Goodman W.K. Cognitive-behavioral therapy for PANDAS-related obsessive-compulsive disorder: findings from a preliminary waitlist controlled open trial. *J Am Acad Child Adolesc Psychiatry.* 2006 Oct;45(10):1171-8.

Stein DG, Wright DW, Kellermann AL. Does progesterone have neuroprotective properties? Ann Emerg Med. 2008 Feb;51(2):164-72.

Tanya VN Tchakouté VL, Graham SP, Jensen SA, Makepeace BL, Nfon CK, Njongmeta LM, Lustigman S, Enyong PA, Bianco AE, Trees AJ. In a bovine model of onchocerciasis, protective immunity exists naturally, is absent in drug-cured hosts, and is induced by vaccination. *Proc Natl Acad Sci U S A.* 2006 Apr 11;103(15):5971-6. Epub 2006 Apr 3.

Tobinick E. Perispinal etanercept for treatment of Alzheimer's disease. Curr Alzheimer Res. 2007 Dec;4(5):550-2.

Tomai M, Kotb M, Majumdar G, et al. Superantigenicity of streptococcalMprotein. *J Exp Med* 1990;172(1):359–62

Trifiletti RR, Packard AM. Immune mechanisms in pediatric neuropsychiatric disorders. Tourette's syndrome, OCD, and PANDAS. *Child Adolesc Psychiatr Clin N Am.* 1999 Oct;8(4):767-75.

Van Ameringen M, Mancini C, Patterson B, Bennett M (2006): Topiramate augmentation in treatment-resistant obsessive-compulsive disorder: a retrospective, open-label case series. *Depression and anxiety* 23:1-5.

Welch JM, Lu J, Rodriguiz RM, Trotta NC, Peca J, Ding JD, Feliciano C, Chen M, Adams JP, Luo J, Dudek SM, Weinberg RJ, Calakos N, Wetsel WC, Feng G. Cortico-striatal synaptic defects and OCD-like behaviours in Sapap3-mutant mice. Nature. 2007 Aug 23;448(7156):894-900.

Wilson, C.J., Finch, C.E., et al., 2002. Cytokines and cognition—the case for a head-to- toe inflammatory paradigm. *J. Am. Geriatr. Soc.* 50 (12), 2041–2056.

Yirmiya R (2000). Depression in medical illness: the role of the immune system. *Western Journal of Medicine* 173, 333–336.

Zai G, Bezchlibnyk YB, Richter MA, et al (2004). Myelin oligodendrocyte glycoprotein (MOG) gene is associated with obsessive-compulsive disorder. *Am J Med Genet B Neuropsychiatr Genet.* 129(1):64–8.

Zhang B, Walsh MD, Nguyen KB, Hillyard NC, Cavanagh AC, McCombe PA, Morton H. (2003). Early pregnancy factor treatment suppresses the inflammatory response and adhesion molecule expression in the spinal cord of SJL/J mice with experimental autoimmune encephalomyelitis and the delayed-type hypersensitivity reaction to trinitrochlorobenzene in normal BALB/c mice. *J Neurol Sci.* Aug 15;212(1-2):37-46.

www.ingramcontent.com/pod-product-compliance
Lightning Source LLC
Chambersburg PA
CBHW072337290526
45794CB00002B/909